TRUE COLORS

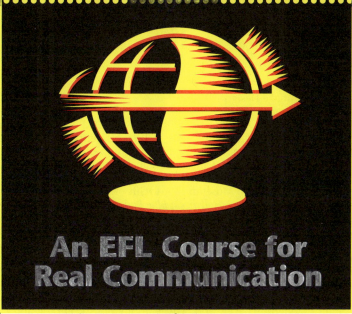

An EFL Course for Real Communication

4

Jay Maurer
Irene E. Schoenberg

Joan Saslow
Series Director

LONGMAN

True Colors: An EFL Course for Real Communication 4

Pearson Education

Editorial director: Allen Ascher
Development editor: Marcia Schonzeit
Director of design and production: Rhea Banker
Production manager: Marie McNamara
Managing editor: Linda Moser
Senior production editors: Christine Cervoni and Michael Kemper
Photo research: Aerin Csigay
Cover design: Rhea Banker
Text design: Word & Image Design
Text composition: Word & Image Design
Senior manufacturing manager: Patrice Fraccio
Text credits: page 80, From: THE POETRY OF ROBERT FROST, edited by Edward Connery Lathem,
    Copyright 1951 by Robert Frost, Copyright 1923, © 1969 by Henry Holt and Company, Inc.,
    © 1997 by Edward Connery Lathem. Reprinted by permission of Henry Holt and Company, Inc.;
    page 83, From COLLECTED POEMS by Langston Hughes. Copyright © 1994 by the Estate of
    Langston Hughes. Reprinted by permission of Alfred A Knopf Inc; page 96, left, Georgia O'Keefe,
    Purple Hills Near Abiquiu. San Diego Museum of Art (Gift of Mr. and Mrs. Norton S. Walbridge).;
    page 96, right, Georgia O'Keefe, *Black Hollyhock, Blue Larkspur*. The Metropolitan Museum of Art,
    George A. Hearn Fund, 1934. (34.51) Photograph by Lynton Gardiner. Photograph © 1987 The
    Metropolitan Museum of Art.; page 97, Georgia O'Keefe, *Cow's Skull: Red, White and Blue*. The
    Metropolitan Museum of Art, Alfred Stieglitz Collection, 1952. (52.203) Photograph © 1994 The
    Metropolitan Museum of Art.; page 101,WYETH, Andrew. *Christina's World*. (1948). Tempera on
    gessoed panel, 32 1/4 x 47 3/4" (81.9 x 121.3 cm). The Museum of Modern Art, New York.
    Purchase. Photograph © 1998 The Museum of Modern Art, New York.; page 101, DALI, Salvador.
    The Persistence of Memory (*Persistance de la mémoire*). 1931. Oil on canvas, 9 1/2 x 13" (24.1 x 33
    cm). The Museum of Modern Art, New York. Given anonymously. Photograph © 1998 The
    Museum of Modern Art, New York.
Text art: Pierre Berthiaume, Jocelyne Bouchard, Nicolas Debon, Patrick Fitzgerald, Stephen
    MacEachern, Jock MacRae, Paul McCusker, Dusan Petricic, Stephen Quinlan, Teco
    Rodrigues, Philip Scheuer
Photo credits: Gilbert Duclos; page 8, Muhammad Ali, Canapress Photo Service; Mother Teresa,
    Canapress Photo Service (Sherwin Crasto); Buddha, Superstock/Steve Vidler; Pope John Paul
    II, Canapress Photo Service (Danilo Schiavella); Julie Andrews, Canapress Photo Service (Jim
    Cooper); Elton John, Superstock/Christopher Harris, page 12, Ken Griffey and Ken Griffey
    Jr., Canapress Photo Service (Scott Troyanos); John F. Kennedy, Superstock/Shostal; Indian
    Prime Minister Jawaharlal Pandit Nehru, Canapress Photo Service; Mata Hari,
    Superstock/Culver Pictures Inc.; George Eliot, copyright Archive Photos; page 44, Panda,
    Canapress Photo Service; page 126, Beatles, Canapress Photo Service (Gael Cornier)

Library of Congress Cataloging-in-Publication Data

Maurer, Jay.
    True colors: an EFL course for real communication/Jay Maurer;
Irene E. Schoenberg; Joan Saslow, series director
        p. cm.
    1. English language—Textbooks for foreign speakers.
2. Communication. I. Schoenberg, Irene. II. Saslow, Joan M. III. Title.

PE1128.M3548   1999

428.2'4–dc21   97-12071
                                                         CIP

ISBN: 0-201-19052-4

2 3 4 5 6 7 8 9 10—WEB—04 03 02 01 00

Contents

Scope and Sequence of Specific Content and Skills

UNIT	Social Language	Grammar and Pronunciation	Listening	Reading
1 **Until then, I'd always loved that name.** page 2	How to: • offer to introduce someone to another person • describe a relationship • make a formal introduction	Grammar: • the past perfect	Type: • conversations Comprehension Skills: • factual recall • determine context • focus attention • listening between the lines	Type: • a photo story Comprehension Skills • inference and interpretation
2 **I guess I shouldn't have yelled at him.** page 14	How to: • express regret • reassure someone	Grammar: • *should have* and *could have* Pronunciation: • reduction	Types: • a photo story • a conversation Comprehension Skills: • inference and interpretation • determine context • listening between the lines	Type: • a magazine article Comprehension Skill • understanding meaning from con
3 **He may have disappeared on purpose.** page 26	How to: • speculate about possibilities • tell someone you took something by mistake	Grammar: • *must have, may have,* and *might have*	Types: • a conversation • a radio quiz program Comprehension Skills: • factual recall • determine context • listening between the lines	Type: • a photo story Comprehension Skill • confirming conten
4 **Should cloning be prohibited?** page 38	How to: • disagree politely • express skepticism about something	Grammar: • the passive voice, review • the passive voice with modals Pronunciation: • the glottal stop	Types: • a photo story • a radio call-in show Comprehension Skills: • understanding meaning from context • determine context • focus attention • listening between the lines	Type: • a magazine article Comprehension Skill • understanding meaning from con
5 **I can have the floors refinished.** page 50	How to: • state a problem • ask for a favor • ask for and give advice about having something done	Grammar: • *make, have, let, help,* and *get* • the passive causative	Type: • conversations Comprehension Skills: • summarizing • determine context • listening between the lines	Type: • a photo story Comprehension Skill • confirming conten
Review of Units 1-5 page 62				
6 **The guy who lives next door blasts music all night long.** page 72	How to: • make a formal complaint • ask for a refund • remind someone of a previous agreement	Grammar: • reduced adjective clauses Pronunciation: • intonation to show interest or lack of interest	Types: • a photo story • a conversation Comprehension Skills: • understanding meaning from context • determine context • listening between the lines	Type: • a magazine article Comprehension Skill • confirming conten • identifying the ma idea
7 **If we hadn't reached him, he would've waited forever.** page 84	How to: • offer help • confirm information • request help in remembering something • respond to a rude question	Grammar: • the past unreal conditional	Type: • conversations Comprehension Skills: • identifying the main idea • understanding meaning from context • focus attention • listening between the lines	Type: • a photo story Comprehension Skill • inference and interpretation
8 **You won't die if you look at some paintings.** page 96	How to: • explain what you like or don't like about something • acknowledge another point of view • arrange a meeting place	Grammar: • adverbial clauses Pronunciation: • rhythm and intonation	Types: • a photo story • conversations Comprehension Skills: • focus attention • listening between the lines	Type: • a newspaper article Comprehension Skill • understanding meaning from context
9 **He said he'd missed his train.** page 108	How to: • express uncertainty about an event's outcome • offer support • express confidence • congratulate someone	Grammar: • quoted and reported speech • verb changes in reported speech • *be supposed to*	Type: • conversations Comprehension Skills: • understanding meaning from context • inference and interpretation • determine context • listening between the lines	Type: • a photo story Comprehension Skill • understanding meaning from context
10 **I'm so tired I don't really feel like going.** page 120	How to: • make an excuse • suggest an alternative • introduce new information	Grammar: • gerunds and infinitives Pronunciation: • the letter "h"	Types: • a photo story • a conversation • a song Comprehension Skills: • understanding meaning from context • determine context • listening between the lines	Type: • a newspaper editor Comprehension Skil • inference and interpretation
Review of Units 6-10 page 132				

Authentic Reading	Writing	Vocabulary	Personal Expression
Type: • a book excerpt from *The Best Baby Name Book* Comprehension Skill: • inference and interpretation	Task: • an essay about one's own name Skill: • prewriting techniques: discussion and brainstorming*	• names	• the interpretation of proverbs • feelings about one's own name
Type: • a true story from *Chicken Soup for the Teenage Soul* Comprehension Skill: • inference and interpretation	Task: • a short narrative Skill: • prewriting technique: freewriting*	• family dynamics	• what people should and shouldn't have done • opinions on expressing regret
Type: • a newspaper article from the *Seattle Post-Intelligencer* Comprehension Skills: • understanding meaning from context • inference and interpretation	Task: • a mystery story Skill: • sequencing*	• all about mystery	• explaining why someone might want to disappear
Type: • a newspaper article from the Associated Press Comprehension Skill: • understanding meaning from context	Task • a business letter Skill: • letter-writing*	• scientific research	• opinions on controversial issues • pros and cons of cloning
Type: • a business magazine article from *Incentive* Comprehension Skill: • confirming content	Task: • an essay about a person who helped others to succeed Skill: • writing supporting details*	• services and people who perform them	• attitudes about asking someone for a favor
Type: • a poem ("Stopping by Woods on a Snowy Evening") Comprehension Skills: • understanding meaning in poetry • inference and interpretation	Tasks: • an essay about a dream or a goal • a story that turns out to be a dream Skill: • outlining*	• sleep and dreams	• how poetry differs from other kinds of writing
Type: • a newspaper article from the Associated Press Comprehension Skills: • factual recall • inference and interpretation	Task: • an essay about a regret Skill: • writing a first draft*	• memory	• the interpretation of a proverb • discussing a relationship
Type: • a book excerpt from *Living with Art* Comprehension Skill: • understanding the main idea	Task: • an essay about a painting Skill: • using peer feedback*	• the importance of art	• reactions to works of art
Type: • a newspaper article from *The New York Times* Comprehension Skill: • inference and interpretation	Task: • an essay about a job Skill: • transitions*	• jobs and employment	• opinions on what makes a good job
Type: • an encyclopedia article from *The New Book of Knowledge* Comprehension Skill: • factual recall	Task: • an essay about a song Skill: • revising*	• music	• the meaning of the *True Colors* song
	* in Teacher's Edition		

Acknowledgments

The authors and series director wish to acknowledge with gratitude the following consultants, reviewers, and piloters—our partners in the development of *True Colors*.

COURSE CONSULTANTS

Berta de Llano, Puebla, Mexico • **Luis Fernando Gómez J.**, School of Education, University of Antioquia, Colombia • **Irma K. Ghosn**, Lebanese American University, Byblos, Lebanon • **Annie Hu**, Fu-Jen Catholic University, Taipei, Taiwan • **Nancy Lake**, CEL-LEP, São Paulo, Brazil • **Frank Lambert**, Pagoda Foreign Language Institute, Seoul, Korea • **Kazuhiko Yoshida**, Kobe University, Kobe City, Japan.

Reviewers and Piloters

Lucia Adrian, EF Language Schools, Miami, Florida, USA • **Ronald Aviles**, Instituto Chileno Norteamericano, Chuquicamata, Chile • **Liliana Baltra**, Instituto Chileno Norteamericano, Santiago, Chile • **Paulo Roberto Berkelmans**, CEL-LEP, São Paulo, Brazil • **Luis Beze**, Casa Thomas Jefferson, Brasília, Brazil • **Martin T. Bickerstaff**, ELS Language Centers, Oakland, California, USA • **Mary C. Black**, Institute of North American Studies, Barcelona, Spain • **James Boyd**, ECC Foreign Language Institute, Osaka, Japan • **Susan Bryan de Martínez**, Instituto Mexicano Norteamericano, Monterrey, Mexico • **Hugo A. Buitano**, Instituto Chileno Norteamericano, Arica, Chile • **Gary Butzbach**, American Language Center, Rabat, Morocco • **Herlinda Canto**, Universidad Popular Autónoma del Estado de Puebla, Mexico • **Rigoberto Castillo**, Colegio de CAFAM, Santafé de Bogotá, Colombia • **Tina M. Castillo**, Santafé de Bogotá, Colombia • **Amparo Clavijo Olarte**, Universidad Distrital, Santafé de Bogotá, Colombia • **Graciela Conocente**, Asociación Mendocina de Intercambio Cultural Argentino Norteamerica, Argentina • **Greg Conquest**, Yokohama Gaigo Business College, Japan • **Eduardo Corbo**, IETI, Salto, Uruguay • **Marilia Costa**, Instituto Brasil-Estados Unidos, Rio de Janeiro, Brazil • **Miles Craven**, Nihon University, Shizuoka, Japan • **Michael Davidson**, EF Language Schools, Miami, Florida, USA • **Celia de Juan**, UNICO, UAG, Guadalajara, Mexico • **Laura de Marín**, Centro Colombo Americano, Medellín, Colombia • **Montserrat Muntaner Djmal**, Instituto Brasil-Estados Unidos, Rio de Janeiro, Brazil • **Deborah Donnelley de García**, ITESM-Campus Querétaro, Mexico • **Rosa Erlichman**, União Cultural, São Paulo, Brazil • **Patricia Escalante Arauz**, Universidad de Costa Rica, San Pedro de Montes de Oca, Costa Rica • **Guadalupe Espinoza**, ITESM-Campus Querétaro, Mexico • **Suad Farkouh**, ESL Consultant to Philadelphia National Schools, Amman, Jordan • **Niura R.H. Ferreria**, Centro Cultural Brasil Estados Unidos, Guarapuava, Brazil • **Fernando Fleurquin**, Alianza Cultural Uruguay-EEUU, Montevideo, Uruguay • **Patricia Fleury**, Casa Thomas Jefferson, Brasília, Brazil • **Patricia Fonceca**, Colegio Jesualdo, Santiago, Chile • **Areta Ulhana Galat**, Centro Cultural Brasil Estados Unidos, Curitiba, Brazil • **Christina Gitsaki**, Nagoya University of Commerce and Business Administration, Japan • **Julie Harris de Peyré**, Universidad del Valle, Guatemala • **Ruth Hassell de Hernández**, UANL, Mexico • **John Hawkes**, EF International School, Santa Barbara, California, USA • **Rose M. Hernández**, University of Puerto Rico-Bayamón, Puerto Rico • **Susan Hills**, EF International School of English, San Diego, California, USA • **Osamu Ikeno**, Ehime University, Japan • **Kevin Johnson**, Sapporo International Junior College, Sapporo, Japan

• **Jan Kelley**, EF International School, Santa Barbara, California, USA • **Mia Kim**, Kyung Hee University, Seoul, Korea • **Junko Kobayashi**, Sankei International College, Tokyo, Japan • **Gil Lancaster**, Academy Istanbul, Istanbul, Turkey • **Loretta Levene**, Southern Illinois University at Carbondale (SIUC), Niigata, Japan • **Amy Rita Lewis**, Keio University, Tokyo, Japan • **Mónica Lobo**, Santiago, Chile • **Luz Adriana Lopera**, Centro Colombo Americano, Medellín, Colombia • **Eva Irene Loya**, ITESM-Campus Querétaro, Mexico • **Mary Maloy Lara**, Instituto John F. Kennedy, Tehuacán, Mexico • **Meire de Jesus Marion**, Associação Alumni, São Paulo, Brazil • **Juliet Marlier**, Universidad de las Américas, Puebla, Mexico • **Yolanda Martínez**, Instituto D'Amicis, Puebla, Mexico • **Neil McClelland**, Shimonoseki City University, Japan • **Regina Celia Pereira Mendes**, Instituto Brasil-Estados Unidos, Rio de Janeiro, Brazil • **Jim Miller**, Yokohama Gaigo Business College, Japan • **Milton Miltiadous**, YMCA College of English, Tokyo, Japan • **Fiona Montarry**, The American Language Center, Casablanca, Morocco • **Luiz Claudio Monteiro**, Casa Thomas Jefferson, Brasília, Brazil • **Angelita Oliveira Moreno**, ICBEU, Belo Horizonte, Brazil • **Ahmed Mohammad Motala**, King Fahd University of Petroleum & Minerals, Dhahran, Saudi Arabia • **William Richard Munzer**, Universidad IDEAS de Bogotá, Colombia • **Akiko Nakazawa**, Yokohama Gaigo Business College, Japan • **Adrian Nunn**, EF International School of English, Los Angeles, California, USA • **Margarita Ordaz Mejía**, Universidad Americana de Acapulco, Mexico • **Sherry Ou**, Fu-Jen Catholic Univ, Taipei, Taiwan • **Thelma Jonas Péres**, Casa Thomas Jefferson, Brasília, Brazil • **Renata Philippov**, Associação Alumni, São Paulo, Brazil • **Ciarán Quinn**, Otemae College, Osaka, Japan • **Ted Quock**, Keisen University, Tokyo, Japan • **Ron Ragsdale**, Bilgi University, Istanbul, Turkey • **Luis Ramírez F.**, Instituto Norteamericano de Cultura, Concepción, Chile • **Martha Restrepo Rodríguez**, Politécnico Grancolombiano, Santafé de Bogotá, Colombia • **Irene Reyes Giordanelli**, Centro Cultural Colombo Americano, Santiago de Cali, Colombia • **Dolores Rodríguez**, CELE (Centro de Lenguas), Universidad Autónoma de Puebla, Mexico • **Idia Rodríguez**, University of Puerto Rico-Arecibo, Puerto Rico • **Eddy Rojas & teachers**, Centro de Idiomas de la P. Universidad Católica, Peru • **Ricardo Romero**, Centro Cultural Colombo Americano, Santafé de Bogotá, Colombia • **Blanca Lilia Rosales Bremont**, Universidad Americana de Acapulco, Mexico • **Stephen Russell**, Tokyo University of Foreign Studies, Tokyo, Japan • **Marie Adele Ryan**, Associação Alumni, São Paulo, Brazil • **Nadia Sarkis**, União Cultural, São Paulo, Brazil • **Andrea Seidel**, Universidad Americana de Acapulco, Mexico • **Hada Shammar**, American Language Center, Amman, Jordan • **Lai Yin Shem**, Centro Colombo Americano, Medellín, Colombia • **Maria Cristina Siqueira**, CEL-LEP, São Paulo, Brazil • **María Inés Sandoval Astudillo**, Instituto Chileno Norteamericano, Chillán, Chile • **Lilian Munhoz Soares**, Centro Cultural Brasil Estados Unidos, Santos, Brazil • **Mário César de Sousa**, Instituto Brasil-Estados Unidos, Fortaleza, Brazil • **Tatiana Suárez**, Politécnico Grancolombiano, Santafé de Bogotá, Colombia • **Richard Paul Taylor**, Nagoya University of Commerce and Business Administration, Japan • **David Thompson**, Instituto Mexicano Norteamericano de Relaciones Culturales, Guadalajara, Mexico • **Yoshihiro Uzawa**, Sankei International College, Tokyo, Japan • **Nilda Valdez**, Centro Cultural Salvadoreño, El Salvador • **Euclides Valencia Cepeda**, Universidad Distrital, Santafé de Bogotá, Colombia • **Ana Verde**, American Language Institute, Montevideo, Uruguay • **Andrea Zaidenberg**, Step English Language Center, Argentina

Preface

●●●

True Colors is a complete and articulated six-level adult or young adult course in English as a foreign language. Each book is intended to be completed in a period of 60 to 90 class hours. There are two reasons why this course is entitled *True Colors*. It presents the true voice of the native speaker of American English, and it systematically teaches students to communicate *in their own words*—to **let their true colors shine through.**

Focus and Approach

True Colors is a highly communicative international course enhanced by strong four-skills support, including an enriched and skills-based listening strand and an abundance of games, info-gaps, and other interactive activities. Short, integrated social language and grammar lessons within each unit ensure concentrated oral practice and production. *True Colors* takes into account different learning and teaching styles. It incorporates task-based strategies and is centered on the well-known fact that practice in each skill area enhances mastery of the others.

A major innovation of the *True Colors* series is to systematically build students' ability to present their own ideas, opinions, and feelings—both accurately and confidently. For this reason, every activity leads students to gain ownership of the language, progressively moving them *away* from models to express thoughts in their own words and to improvise based on what they know.

True Colors carefully distinguishes between receptive and productive language. It consistently presents language in the receptive mode before—and at a slightly higher difficulty level than—the productive mode. Research has shown that students are more successful when they become familiar with new language before having to produce it. Therefore, *True Colors* presents EFL students with an abundance of both receptive and productive models, combining exposure and practice for increased understanding and attainable mastery.

True Colors is specifically designed for use by students who rarely encounter English outside of class. The course is built around a wealth of speaking and reading models of the true voice of the American speaker and includes numerous authentic readings from English-language newspapers, encyclopedias, magazines, books, and poetry. This refreshing change from "textbook English" is essential for students who have limited access to real native speech and writing.

Because international students do not have the opportunity to speak to native speakers on a regular basis, *True Colors* does not present activities such as interviewing native speakers or watching TV in English. Instead, the course serves as a replacement for immersion in an English-speaking environment, making the classroom itself a microcosm of the English-speaking world. The goal and promise of *True Colors* is to prepare students to move out of this textbook and to understand, speak, read, and write English in the real world.

Student Population

Book 1 of *True Colors* is written for adult and young adult false beginners. Book 2 is written at a high-beginning to low-intermediate level. Book 3 is at an intermediate level, Book 4 is at a high-intermediate level, and Book 5 concludes at an advanced level. The Basic text is an alternative entry point for true beginners or very weak false beginners.

Course Length

The *True Colors* student's books are designed to cover from 60 to 90 class hours of instruction. Although each student's book is a complete course in itself, giving presentation, practice, and production of all four skills, a full complement of supplementary components is available to further expand the material.

Components of the Course

Student's Book The student's book is made up of ten units and two review units, one coming after Unit 5 and another coming after Unit 10.

Teacher's Edition The teacher's edition is interleaved with the full-color student's book pages. It contains an introduction to the format and approach of *True Colors*; page-by-page teaching suggestions written especially for the teacher who teaches outside an English-speaking country; tapescripts for the audiocassettes or audio CDs; and a complete answer key to the exercises in the student's book, workbook, and achievement tests.

Teacher's Bonus Pack The Teacher's Bonus Pack is a unique set of reproducible hands-on learning-support activities that includes duplicating masters that contain photo stories with empty speech balloons for oral and written improvisation; full-page art illustrations that recombine and recycle vocabulary, grammar, and social language from many units; learner-created grammar notes; and interactive conversation cards for social language reinforcement. The Teacher's Bonus Pack contains an array of opportunities to expand the student's book and tailor it to each classroom's particular needs.

Workbook The workbook contains numerous additional opportunities for written reinforcement of the language taught in the student's book. The exercises in the workbook are suitable for homework or for classwork.

Audiocassettes or Audio CDs The audiocassettes or audio CDs contain all the listening and reading texts, the conversations, the vocabulary presentations, the Listening with a Purpose texts, the Authentic Readings, and the pronunciation presentations and practices from the student's book. The cassettes and CDs provide space for student practice and self-correction.

Videocassette The videocassette, *True Voices*, contains a unique combination of controlled dramatic episodes that support the social language and grammar in the *True Colors* student's book; excerpts from real television broadcasts; and authentic, unrehearsed discussions by ordinary people on a variety of subjects introduced in the student's book unit.

Video Workbook A video workbook enhances comprehension and provides active language practice and reinforcement of all social language and grammar from the video.

Achievement Tests Achievement tests offer opportunities for evaluation of student progress on a unit-by-unit basis and provide a midterm and a final test as well. In addition, a placement test is available to aid in placing groups or individuals in one of the six levels of *True Colors*: Basic, Book 1, Book 2, Book 3, Book 4, or Book 5.

Student's Book Unit Contents

Photo Story An illustrated conversation or story provokes interest, provides enjoyment, and demonstrates the use of target language in authentic, natural speech. This rich model of real speech can be presented as a reading or a listening. It is purposely designed to be a slight step ahead of students' productive ability because students can understand more than they can produce, and the EFL student needs abundant authentic models of native speech.

Comprehension Activities based on the photo story focus on the key comprehension skills of factual recall, confirmation of content, identifying main ideas, inference and interpretation, and understanding meaning from context. These activities can serve as listening comprehension or reading comprehension exercises. Additionally, students have an opportunity to express personal opinions about an aspect of the photo story or to retell the photo story to a partner, in their own words.

Grammar and Meaning A reading or listening text provides a richly contextualized presentation of the unit's grammar while introducing the theme of the unit.

Comprehension An exercise ensures comprehension of the reading or listening focus and prepares the way for the grammar presentation to follow.

Grammar presentation A concise but clearly explained presentation of the unit's target grammar provides rules for meaning and use as well as representative examples that help all types of students learn the grammar. The grammar presentations anticipate the social language and support the unit's thematic focus. Grammar therefore is never taught in isolation, but rather forms a support for the social language and thematic focus of the unit, giving the grammar both meaning and purpose. To this end, grammar exercises are set in a context that supports the communicative focus of the unit.

Social Language Lessons Short, numbered lessons form the social language core of each unit of *True Colors*. Social language and grammar are woven through each of these "mini-lessons" through the following combination of presentations and opportunities for practice:

Conversation A short dialogue at the students' productive level presents and models important social language.

 A major goal of *True Colors* is to teach students to improvise based on the language they already know. Improvisation is the "fifth skill"—the one students need to master in order to move out of the pages of a textbook and into the real world. Improvise activities expand the Conversation, allowing for personalization and the incorporation of new contexts and situations.

Pronunciation Five of the ten units include a pronunciation section that isolates an important feature of the pronunciation or intonation of spoken American English. The emphasis is on practice of these features, and each is supported by recorded examples on the audiocassettes or audio CDs.

Game or Inter-Action Each unit contains at least one interactive language activity that activates grammar, social language, vocabulary, or pronunciation.

Listening with a Purpose In addition to the other recorded texts in the unit, one or two additional listening texts provide another receptive model a step above students' productive ability. A three-step comprehension syllabus centers on three essential listening skills—determining context, focusing attention, and listening between the lines. Through a unique and rigorous approach to listening comprehension that is similar to the reading comprehension skills of skimming, scanning, and inferring, students build their ability to understand at a level above what is normally expected of intermediate-level students.

Authentic Reading Each unit provides practice in reading authentic texts from a variety of sources: newspapers, books, magazines, brochures, poetry, and encyclopedias. Selections are chosen to expand the thematic focus of the unit, to provide material to support and motivate discussion and writing, and to prepare students to cope with authentic materials. Each authentic reading is followed by further comprehension practice in reading comprehension sub-skills.

 This unique and exciting culminating activity systematically builds students' ability to express their own opinions, ideas, and feelings on a variety of topics. Carefully designed questions provoke interest without soliciting production above students' level. Each Heart to Heart activity comes at a place where students have had enough preparation for success.

Vocabulary Vocabulary sections present thematically related vocabulary to enhance students' discussions, interactions, and writings. The words are presented in a variety of ways: through pictures, with definitions, and through contextual sentences. These presentations ensure comprehension and provide students with a model for defining and explaining new words in the future.

 **Speaking** This full-page illustration that ends each unit has been especially drawn to elicit from students all the language they have learned within the unit—the vocabulary, the social language, the grammar, and the thematic contexts. Students can ask each other questions about the actions depicted, make true and false statements about what they see, create conversations for the characters, tell stories about what is happening—all IN THEIR OWN WORDS. All students, regardless of ability, will succeed at their own levels because what the students know how to say has been included in the illustration. What they don't know how to say has been purposely left out. Furthermore, because language learning is a process of continuing activation, the In Your Own Words illustrations include opportunities to recycle and reuse vocabulary, grammar, and social language from previous units as well.

Writing Writing activities in each unit provide real and realistic writing tasks. At the same time they offer practice in paragraph and composition development that reinforces the target language while providing additional opportunities for personal expression.

Review Units These units are provided mid-book, after Unit 5, and at the end. They provide review, self-tests, extra classroom practice, and a social language self-test.

Appendices The key vocabulary, verb charts, adjective and adverb charts, and grammatical terms are organized and presented at the end of the book for easy reference and test preparation.

About the Authors and Series Director

Authors

Jay Maurer

Jay Maurer has taught English in Binational Centers, colleges, and universities in Portugal, Spain, Mexico, the Somali Republic, and the United States. In addition, he taught intensive English at Columbia University's American Language Program.

Dr. Maurer has an M.A. and an M. Ed. in Applied Linguistics as well as a Ph. D. in The Teaching of English, all from Columbia University. In addition to this new adult and young adult English course, he is the author of the Advanced Level of Longman's widely acclaimed *Focus on Grammar* series, coauthor of the three-level *Structure Practice in Context* series, and coauthor of the *True Voices* video series. Dr. Maurer teaches and writes in the Seattle, Washington, area and recently conducted a series of teaching workshops in Brazil and Japan.

Irene E. Schoenberg

Irene E. Schoenberg has taught English to international students for over twenty years at Hunter College's International Language Institute and at Columbia University's American Language Program. Additionally, she trains English instructors in EFL/ESL teaching methods at The New School for Social Research. Her M.A. is in TESOL from Columbia University. She is a popular speaker to national and international TESOL groups.

Professor Schoenberg is the author of the Basic Level of the *Focus on Grammar* series as well as the author of the two engaging, unique, and widely used conversation texts, *Talk About Trivia* and *Talk About Values*. In addition to *True Colors*, Professor Schoenberg has coauthored the *True Voices* video series.

Series Director

Joan Saslow

Joan Saslow has taught English and foreign languages to adults and young adults in both South America and the United States. She taught English at the Binational Centers of Valparaíso and Viña del Mar, Chile, and English and French at the Catholic University of Valparaíso. She taught English to Japanese university students at Marymount College and to international students in Westchester Community College's intensive program.

Ms. Saslow, whose B.A. and M.A. are from the University of Wisconsin, is author of *English in Context: Reading Comprehension for Science and Technology*, a three-level series. In addition, she has been an editor of language teaching materials, a teacher trainer, and a frequent speaker at gatherings of English teachers outside the United States for twenty-five years.

Until then, I'd always loved that name.

Warm up: *Do you like your name? Is there another name you'd rather have? Read or listen.* 🎧

Ted, I've got this list of French names here. Could you take a minute to help me pick one out?

So you're really serious about taking a French name for your year in France?

I guess I am. I just don't want to spend a whole year there with the name Ginger.

Well, I think changing your name is a silly idea, but let me have a look.

Hmm. How does Genevieve strike you? It starts with a "G."

Too long.

Too long . . . OK. What about Gigi? It sounds sort of like Ginger.

Uh-uh. I need a more serious name.

Serious. . . . Serious. . . . I've got it . . . Gisele.

Nope. I could never use the name Gisele.

Wow, are you hard to please! What's wrong with Gisele?

Well, Gisele's actually a beautiful name, and I'd always loved it . . . that is, until I worked for a Gisele. . . . No, I'm afraid Gisele's out.

Yeah, names can be funny sometimes. What's wrong with Ginger, anyway?

Nothing, really. It's just that the last time I was in the Paris office, nobody could pronounce it.

By the end of the first week, I'd been called every name in the book—from Jeanne Jaire to Sheen Share.

And that's why you want a new name?

No. It's more than that. The year in Paris means a lot to me. I want to try and do all sorts of new things. I think a new name will help.

Personally, I wouldn't change my name for all the money in the world. I disagree with that old saying, "A rose by any other name would smell as sweet."

Comprehension: Inference and Interpretation

Answer the following questions.

1. What do you think Ginger means when she says, "I'm afraid Gisele's out"?
2. What do you think this means: "A rose by any other name would smell as sweet"?
3. Which speaker probably believes the proverb, "When in Rome, do as the Romans do"—Ginger, Ted, or both?

 **Tell a partner about Ginger. What does she want to do? Why? Use your own words. Say as much as you can.**

GRAMMAR AND MEANING

The past perfect

Receptive Model

Listening Focus • A Conversation

***B**efore You Listen:* Why do people have nicknames?

🎧 Listen to the conversation about real names and nicknames.

Comprehension: Factual Recall 1

🎧 Listen to the conversation again. Each person in the conversation has a nickname and a real name. As you listen, complete the chart.

Nickname	Real Name
Cookie	
Mandy	
Tex	
Dan	

Comprehension: Factual Recall 2

🎧 Now listen again. This time listen specifically for the reasons the speakers give for their nicknames. Then complete each sentence by circling the correct letter.

1. Cookie got her nickname because _____.

    a. no one could pronounce her real name   **b.** she was angry at her parents   **c.** she was always saying the word *cookie*

2. Mandy got her nickname because _____.

    a. she didn't like her real name   **b.** she wanted a less formal name   **c.** she wanted a more formal name

3. Tex got his nickname because _____.

    a. people laughed at his real name   **b.** his real name was too hard to spell   **c.** his real name was too long

4. Dan uses his nickname because _____.

    a. his real name is difficult to pronounce   **b.** short names are popular   **c.** he doesn't like his real name

TAREA

The Past Perfect

Use the simple past tense to describe events that occurred at a specific time in the past.

> I **called** you last night.

Use the past perfect to show that something happened before a specific time in the past. Use the past perfect with the simple past tense to show which of two events happened first.

> By the time you **called** me, I **had** already **left**. (= I left before you called me.)

By and **by the time** are often used in sentences that include the past perfect.

To form the past perfect, use **had** + past participle.

>   **had**   past participle
> We visited Paris last summer. We **had** never **been** there before.

GRAMMAR TASK: Find an example of the past perfect in the photo story on pages 2–3. What are the two past events? Which came first?

Grammar in a Context: Verb Tense Review

Today was Jack's first day in class after vacation. Complete his story using the past perfect and other verb forms. Circle the correct verb forms.

Today was my first day back in class after vacation. I (**1.** get / got) up a bit late and (**2.** haven't had / didn't have) time for breakfast. I (**3.** 'm not / wasn't) concerned because I often (**4.** eat / was eating) at school. However, when I (**5.** get / got) to the bus stop, the bus (**6.** used to leave / had just left). That meant I (**7.** 'm going to miss / was going to miss) breakfast altogether.

At school I (**8.** 'm meeting / met) our new teacher. By then I (**9.** was / have been) very hungry. I (**10.** remember / remembered) I (**11.** had put / was putting) a candy bar in my book bag, so I (**12.** start / started) looking for it. Just then the teacher (**13.** ask / asked) me a question, but I wasn't paying attention, so he asked Clara, my partner, my name. Clara (**14.** had forgotten / was forgetting) my last name. She said, "He's Jack . . . uh Superman." Suddenly all eyes (**15.** have been / were) on me. I quickly corrected Clara, "Not Superman, Zuckerman." But it was too late. Since that time everyone (**16.** has been calling / called) me Superman. At first I was embarrassed, but now I (**17.** 'm beginning / begin) to like my nickname. Maybe I (**18.** 'm changing / 'll change) it officially. Who knows? What do you think?

Jack M. Superman

Grammar in a Context

Complete the sentences. Use the simple past tense and the past perfect.

_____ you _____ through to your doctor?
1. get

Well yes, but her receptionist _____ me on hold for fifteen minutes. I _____
2. keep
3. be
so mad that by the time I _____ to the doctor, I _____ half my questions.
4. speak
5. forget

Grammar with a Partner

Tell your partner about your early life or the early life of a person you know. Use the past perfect.

Example: By the time my best friend was fifteen, he had been to six different schools.

SOCIAL LANGUAGE 1
HOW TO offer to introduce someone to another person/ describe a relationship

Conversation

🎧 *Read and listen to the conversation.*

A: That's our new boss over there near the door. Let me introduce you to him.
B: Do you know him well?
A: We're not on a first-name basis, but we've met several times.
B: What's he like?
A: He's great. I'm sure you'll like him.

🎧 *Listen again and practice.*

☑ **Now you know how to offer to introduce someone to another person. You also know how to describe a relationship.**

HOW TO **make a formal introduction**

Conversation

🎧 *Read and listen to the conversation.*

A: Bob, I'd like to introduce you to Roger Lee. Roger is our new marketing manager. Roger, this is Bob Greenfield, head of our legal department.

B: Hi, Roger. It's a pleasure to meet you.

C: Nice to meet you, too.

🎧 *Listen again and practice.*

Improvise

Improvise a conversation with three people. You are at a formal gathering such as a business reception or a conference.

Tell your partner about one of the other people there. Then introduce your partner to that person. Use the conversations as models.

Some Ideas

the new boss

the guest speaker

the host / hostess

the new head of marketing

the artist

or your OWN idea

☑ **Now you know how to make a formal introduction.**

 **Inter-Action** *(reinforces the past perfect and other verb tenses)*

Partner B, turn to page 142.

Partner A, read these sentences about famous people to Partner B.

Partner B, read a matching sentence that identifies each of the six famous people.

Example: **Partner A:** Agnes Gonxha Bojaxhiu was born in Macedonia in 1910 and died in Calcutta in 1997.

Partner B: By the time Mother Teresa was awarded the Nobel Peace Prize in 1979, she had already been helping the poor in India for thirty-one years.

Muhammad Ali

Mother Teresa

Buddha

Pope John Paul II

Julie Andrews

Elton John

Partner A's Sentences

1. Julia Wells, born in Walton, England, in 1935, showed talent for music when she was a child.

2. Siddarta Gautama, born in India in 563 B.C., had been a prince during the early part of his life but left his family at the age of twenty-nine.

3. Future songwriter and performer Reginald Dwight was born in Middlesex, England, in 1947.

4. Cassius Clay, born in Louisville, Kentucky, in 1942, began boxing at an early age.

5. Karol Wojtyla was born in Krakow, Poland, in 1920 and was ordained as a priest in 1946.

6. Agnes Gonxha Bojaxhiu was born in Macedonia in 1910 and died in Calcutta in 1997.

Now complete the chart with your partner.

Original Name	Name Commonly Known By
Agnes Gonxha Bojaxhiu	*Mother Teresa*
Julia Wells	
Cassius Clay	
Siddarta Gautama	
Reginald Dwight	
Karol Wojtyla	

Listening with a Purpose

Determine Context

🎧 *Listen to the conversation. Then answer each question in your own words.*

"**What's in a name? A rose by any other name would smell as sweet.**"

1. What is the relationship between the speakers? _____

2. Where are they? _____

3. What is the occasion? _____

Focus Attention

🎧 *Listen again to the conversation. Then complete each statement in Column A by circling the correct verb.*

A

1. The man (has / hasn't) been a football player.

2. The man (likes / doesn't like) the name Shelly.

3. The woman (wants / doesn't want) to name the child Thor.

4. The woman (likes / doesn't like) the name Quentin.

B

a. "That's a girl's name."

b. "It's not too common, either."

c. "Just like his dad."

d. "You've got to be kidding."

e. "It definitely sounds strong."

f. "It's unusual."

g. "It sounds like the name of a superhero."

Listening Between the Lines

🎧 *Now listen between the lines. Match each statement in Column A with a quotation in Column B that supports your choice. You will not use all the quotations in Column B.*

I'm against...

It depends.

In my opinion...

I'm for...

Talk with a partner. What are some first names that you particularly like or don't like? Why?

I don't feel strongly about...

As far as I'm concerned...

What about you?

Authentic Reading

from *The Best Baby Name Book*

Before You Read: *How do our names affect the way other people think of us?*
Read this excerpt. 🎧

PENSANDObb   SIAM PENSARb

Stereotypes of Names

Consciously or unconsciously, we all have private pictures of the people who answer to certain names. Jackie could be sophisticated and beautiful, like Jackie Kennedy, or fat and funny, like Jackie Gleason. These pictures come from personal experience as well as from the images we absorb from the mass media and thus may conflict in interesting ways. Marilyn may be the personification of voluptuous femininity until you think of your neighbor who fetches the mail in a ratty bathrobe, with curlers in her hair and a cigarette dangling out of her mouth.

Over the years researchers have been fascinated by the "real" meanings of names and their effects on their bearers. Studies indicate that people actually tend to agree on each name's characteristics.

If people think of Mallory as cute and likable, does that influence a girl named Mallory to become cute and likable? Experts agree that names don't guarantee instant success or condemn people to certain failure, but they *do* affect self-images, influence relationships with others, and help (or hinder) success in work and school.

Researcher S. Gray Garwood conducted a study of sixth graders in New Orleans. He found that students given names that were popular with teachers scored higher in skills tests, were better adjusted and more consistent in their self-perceptions, were more realistic in their evaluations of themselves, and more frequently expected to attain their goals—even though their goals were more ambitious than ones set by their peers.

In San Diego, research suggested that average essays by Davids, Michaels, Karens, and Lisas got better grades than average essays written by Elmers, Huberts, Adelles, and Berthas. The reason? Teachers expected kids with popular names to do better, and thus they assigned higher grades to those kids in a self-fulfilling prophecy.

The name you select for your baby is likely to be that child's "label" for a lifetime. It is important to consider how that name will be perceived by others before making your final choice.

Source: © 1979, 1984 by Bruce Lansky. Reprinted from *The Best Baby Name Book* by permission of the publisher Meadowbrook Press, Minnetonka, MN.

Comprehension: Inference and Interpretation

Complete each statement by circling one of the choices below, according to the author's meaning and point of view.

1. When we hear a person's name before we meet the person, _____.

a. we rarely imagine what that person will look like

b. we often imagine the person will be much better looking than the person is

c. we often have a picture of what that person will look like

2. The author of this article thinks _____.

a. you should give your child a short name

b. you should carefully consider the consequences of any name you give your child

c. you should give your child an unusual name

Vocabulary

Names

🎧 *Say each word or phrase. Study the definitions.*

a given name: A person's given name is that person's first name.

  Tony Blair's **given name** is Tony.

a surname: A person's surname is that person's last or family name.

  Nelson Mandela's **surname** is Mandela.

a middle name: A middle name is a name between the first name and the last name.

  Wolfgang Amadeus Mozart's **middle name** was Amadeus.

a pseudonym: A pseudonym, or pen name, is a name used by writers who do not want to use their real name.

  Samuel Clemens's **pseudonym** was Mark Twain.

a nickname: A nickname is a special name often used instead of a given name.

  When I was a child, my **nickname** was Red because I had red hair.

a title: A title is a formal attachment—for example, *doctor* or *professor*—to a person's name, usually given as a sign of respect.

  Sigmund Freud's **title** was Dr. Freud.

named after, named for: A person who is named after (for) another person has the same name as that person. This is usually done to honor the original person.

  I was **named after (for)** my grandfather on my mother's side.

senior: The word *senior* placed after a man's name means that he has a son with exactly the same given name.

  Clifford Taylor **Sr.** was born in Boston, Massachusetts, in 1940.

junior: The word *junior* placed after a man's name means that he has a father with exactly the same given name.

  Clifford Taylor **Jr.** was born in Washington, D.C., in 1971.

for short: The phrase *for short* attached to a name means that the name is a shorter form of a longer name.

  We named our son Daniel, or Dan **for short.**

an alias: An alias is a special name used by someone who does not wish his or her real name to be known.

  Detectives, spies, and criminals often go by **aliases.**

Vocabulary Practice

Look at the pictures. Fill in each blank with the correct vocabulary item.
Use each word or phrase only once.

Ken Griffey, 1969– **Ken Griffey, 1950–**

These men are both famous baseball players. Ken

Griffey _____Jr_____ is the man on

the left. Ken Griffey _____Sr_____ is

the man on the right. The younger man was

_____NAMED AFTER_____ his father.
3.

**John F. Kennedy,
1917–1963**

U.S. President John F. Kennedy was often called

Jack, his _____NICKNAME_____.
4.

**Indian Prime Minister
Jawaharlal Pandit Nehru,
1889–1964**

This person's _____TITLE_____ is Prime Minister. His
5.

_____SURNAME_____ is Nehru. His _____given_____
6.   7.

is Jawaharlal. His _____MIDDLE NAME_____ is Pandit.
8.

Margarete Gertrud Zelle, who went by the _____Alias_____
9.

Mata Hari, was a famous Dutch spy during World War I.

Mata Hari, 1876–1917

**Lady Diana Spencer,
1961–1997**

Princess Diana, Lady Diana Spencer, was often

called Di _____For short_____.
10.

English novelist Mary Ann Evans went by the _____pseudanymn_____
11.

George Eliot.

George Eliot, 1819–1880

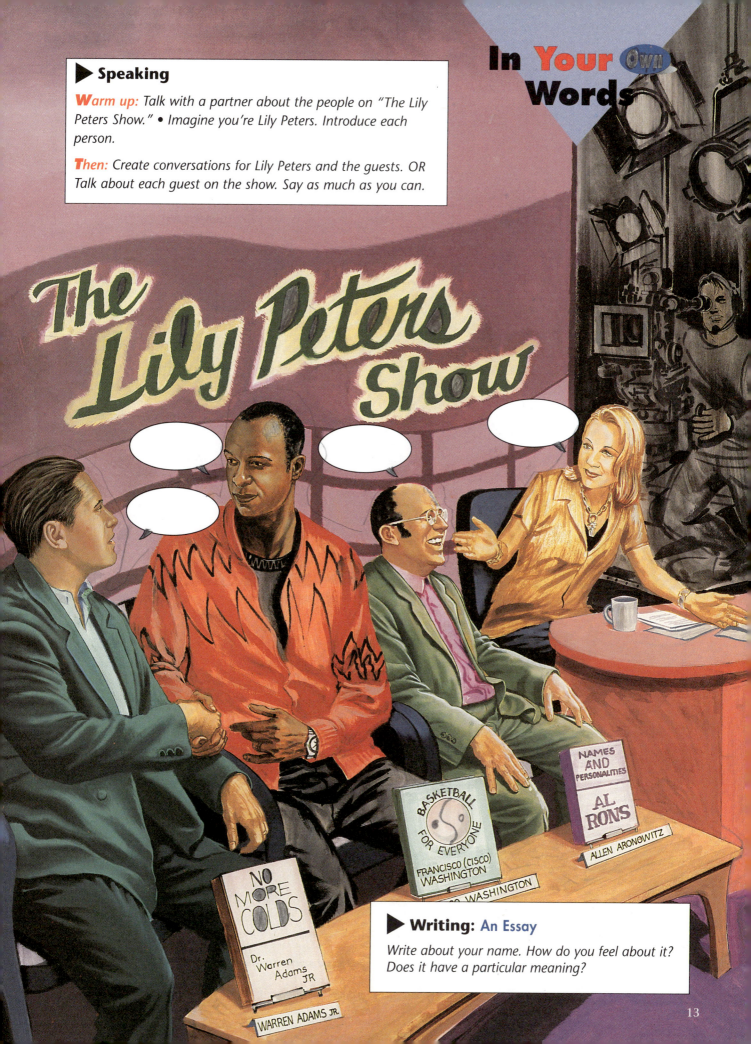

▶ **Speaking**

Warm up: Talk with a partner about the people on "The Lily Peters Show." • Imagine you're Lily Peters. Introduce each person.

Then: Create conversations for Lily Peters and the guests. OR Talk about each guest on the show. Say as much as you can.

▶ **Writing: An Essay**

Write about your name. How do you feel about it? Does it have a particular meaning?

I guess I shouldn't have yelled at him.

Warm up: Why do you think parents and teenagers have trouble communicating? Listen. 🎧

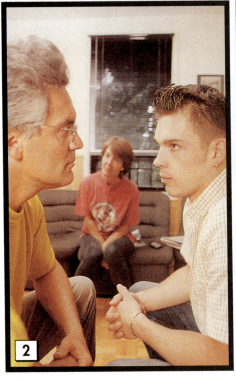

5

6

Comprehension: Inference and Interpretation

🎧 *Listen to the conversation again. Then complete each sentence by circling the correct letter.*

1. The son probably gets along better with _____.

   a. his father   **b.** his mother

2. According to the rules in this family, Trevor needs to call his parents if _____.

   a. he is going to be late for a meal   **b.** he is going to play volleyball

3. The father _____ earrings for boys.

   a. doesn't like   **b.** likes

4. The mother thinks her husband _____.

   a. handled the situation with Trevor very well   **b.** didn't handle the situation with Trevor very well

5. Trevor has _____ brother.

   a. an older   **b.** a younger

6. At the end of the conversation, the father _____ about the way he handled the situation with Trevor.

   a. isn't sorry   **b.** is sorry

Tell a partner about the problem in Trevor's family. Use your own words. Say as much as you can.

Should have and could have

Reading Focus • A Magazine Article

Before You Read: What do you think creates a child's personality and character?

Read the article. (Note the examples of **should have** and **could have** in bold type.) 🎧

Psychology Tomorrow   **July**

Like Father, Like Son— But Not Like Brother

by Madeleine McGowan, Ph.D.

Do you think you've got your children completely figured out? Well, maybe you do. But maybe you shouldn't be so sure.

Consider the case of Julia and Rick Holloway. Four years after their daughter Rhonda was born, Julia and Rick had a second daughter, whom they named Kate. Getting Rhonda through her first four years had been a relatively peaceful task, and they felt they were up to the challenge of a second child. They figured that raising Kate would be pretty much like raising Rhonda. They just assumed that Kate would be similar to her sister. Wrong!

Kate turned out to be very different from Rhonda. Rhonda, for instance, would always do little chores that her parents asked her to do, such as making her bed or picking up her toys.

Kate refused to do them. Rhonda had always been quite obedient, but it seemed that Kate rebelled against almost everything her parents wanted her to do. Rhonda usually wanted to play alone, but Kate usually enjoyed the company of other children. At first Julia and Rick were puzzled. As time went on, they got more and more frustrated because they didn't know how to handle Kate.

How can we account for the difference between these two children and, for that matter, between any brothers and sisters? One possible explanation given by certain psychologists and other researchers is the theory of birth order. According to this theory, birth order plays a large role in determining the personality and character of a child. Firstborn children have an advantage with their parents simply because they were born first. When second, third, and later children come along, they have to do something to get their parents' attention and earn their love. The way they usually do this is to become different from their older brother or sister. Supporters of the birth order theory say that, while not all firstborn children behave the same, firstborns in general tend to be obedient and conservative, sharing their parents' values. Later-born children tend to be more liberal, individual, and rebellious.

Not everyone accepts the birth order theory. Opponents of the theory say that too many individuals simply don't fit the pattern. Instead of being conservative and obedient, some firstborns are rebellious and individualistic, and some laterborns are obedient and conservative. Many opponents of the birth order theory argue that the most important cause of behavior is genetics. Children inherit characteristics from their ancestors, and birth order, they say, has relatively little to do with their personality and character.

Meanwhile, what about the case of Julia and Rick Holloway and their second daughter, Kate? When Kate was fifteen, things reached their lowest point. She got into trouble in school and was even arrested for shoplifting from a local store. She fought constantly with her parents. For a two-year period, life with Kate was very difficult. Julia and Rick felt terrible about themselves, wondering what they had done wrong. Rick said, "Remember that time when she was six years old and wanted a pet? Maybe we **shouldn't have said** no." Both Julia and Rick said, "We **could have done** a better job of raising her." But then, when Kate was seventeen, things changed. Kate changed. Suddenly she became responsible. She was no longer disobedient or rebellious. She did well in school. She got herself a part-time job. Julia and Rick **shouldn't have worried** so much, for Kate turned out well.

So have you got your children all figured out? Perhaps you do. On the other hand, maybe you don't. Perhaps author Henry James had it right when he said, "Never say you know the last word about any human heart."

Comprehension: Understanding Meaning from Context

Circle the choice closest in meaning to each underlined word or phrase.

1. Kate <u>rebelled against almost everything her parents wanted her to do</u>.

   a. obeyed her parents   **b.** did not obey her parents   **c.** didn't understand what her parents wanted

2. How can we <u>account for</u> the difference between these children and, for that matter, between any brothers or sisters?

   a. count   **b.** explain   **c.** pay for

3. Firstborns in general <u>tend to be</u> obedient and conservative.

   a. are always   **b.** aren't usually   **c.** are usually

4. Rhonda would always do little <u>chores</u> that her parents asked her to do, such as making her bed or picking up her toys.

   a. jobs   **b.** games   **c.** differences

5. Kate got into trouble in school and was even arrested for <u>shoplifting</u> from a local store.

   a. stealing things   **b.** buying things   **c.** ordering things

Should Have and Could Have

Use **should have** + past participle to make judgments about the past.

>   *should have   past participle*
>
> I know I **should have called,** but I was tied up at a meeting.
>
> I'm exhausted. I **shouldn't have gone** to bed so late.

Use **could have** + past participle to describe a past opportunity or possibility.

>   *could have   past participle*
>
> You **could have handled** it a little better.

A sentence with **should have** or **could have** generally means that the action didn't happen.

> We **could've gone** to Hawaii. (= We didn't go.)

A sentence with **shouldn't have** generally means that the action did happen.

> I **shouldn't have yelled** at him. (= I did yell at him.)

GRAMMAR TASK: Find a statement that expresses a past opportunity in the Reading Focus on pages 16–17.

Grammar in a Context

*Complete the conversation. Use **should've** or **could've** and the appropriate form of the indicated verbs.*

It was a wonderful party, Helen.

Thanks. I _____
1. not, do
it alone. You were a great help.

How many people came, do you think?

About fifty. Tell me, do you think I _____ Bob's ex-wife?
2. invite
We all used to be very close.

No. I think you were right not to include her. It _____ a really awkward situation.
3. be

Grammar with a Partner

Tell your partner about something you shouldn't have done. Then tell how you could have handled the situation in a different way.

Example: I was cooking dinner when I decided to call my best friend. I wasn't paying attention to my cooking, so I burned a good pot. I guess I shouldn't have tried to talk on the phone and cook at the same time. I could have called her later.

Game *(reinforces should have and could have)*

Play in groups. Look at each situation. Think of as many ways as possible that the problem could have or should have been avoided. The group gets one point for each solution. Share solutions with the class. The group with the most points wins.

Examples: I could've called the host before the party. *or*
I should've worn jeans like everyone else. *or*
I could've said I was coming from a wedding.

I overslept!

I lost my wallet!

I missed the bus!

Boy, did I wear the wrong clothes!

SOCIAL LANGUAGE 1

How to express regret

Conversation

🎧 *Read and listen to the conversation.*

A: I owe my assistant an apology.
B: Why?
A: I got really angry when he forgot to mail some letters.
B: Well, you had a right to be upset.
A: I know, but I shouldn't have yelled at him. I feel awful.
B: Just <u>tell him you're sorry</u>. He'll forgive you.
A: Good idea. I'll give him a call right now.

🎧 *Listen again and practice.*

☑ **Now you know how to express regret.**

Variations

tell him you're sorry
apologize

I GUESS I SHOULDN'T HAVE YELLED AT HIM. **19**

HOW TO reassure someone

Conversation

🎧 *Read and listen to the conversation.*

A: I really should have watched my temper with Sally. I had no idea she had lost her job.

B: Don't let it get to you. You couldn't have known.

A: I guess you're right.

🎧 *Listen again and practice.*

Improvise a conversation in which you feel bad for getting angry with a friend who's having a problem. Your partner reassures you. Use the conversation as a model.

Some Ideas

- Someone lost a job.
- Someone has been sick.
- Someone has gotten divorced.
- Someone has had a death in the family.

or your OWN idea

☑ **Now you know how to reassure someone.**

Pronunciation

Reduction

*In sentences with **should have** and **could have, have** is not stressed. It is normally pronounced like "of."*

🎧 *Listen to these examples:*

You should've come to the party.
You could've called me.

🎧 *Read and listen to the following sentences.*

1. We should've put the shoes in the closet.

2. She could've come alone.

3. I shouldn't have cut the cake.

4. He couldn't have known the answer.

🎧 *Listen again and repeat. Be sure to reduce **have** to make it sound like "of."*

Authentic Reading

from *Chicken Soup for the Teenage Soul*

Before You Read: *Regrets can be painful. Do you have any regrets?*

This story was written by Nick Curry III, a young man whose parents own a funeral home. Read excerpts of his story.

I Love You, Dad

I met a man who came to Tampa for his father's funeral. Father and son hadn't seen each other in years. In fact, according to the son, his father had left when he was a boy, and they had had little contact until about a year ago, when his father had sent him a birthday card with a note saying he'd like to see his son again.

After discussing a trip to Florida with his wife and children and consulting his busy schedule at the office, the son tentatively set a date to visit his father two months later.

It just so happened that the man's daughter made the cheerleading squad at her school and had to go to a camp conducted for cheerleading techniques. Coincidentally, it started the week after school was out. The trip to Florida would have to be postponed.

His father said he understood, but the son didn't hear from him again for some time.

In November the son received a call from his father's neighbor. His father had been taken to the hospital with heart problems. The son spoke with the nurse, who assured him his father was doing well following a heart attack.

His father said, "I'm fine. You don't have to make a trip out here."

He called his father every few days after that. They chatted and laughed and talked about getting together "soon." He sent money for Christmas. His father sent small gifts for his children and a pen and pencil set for his son. But his wife received a precious music box made of crystal. Overwhelmed, she expressed her gratitude to the old man when they called him on Christmas Day. "It was my mother's," the old man explained. "I wanted you to have it."

The man's wife told her husband that they should have invited the old man for the holidays. As an excuse for not having done so, she added, "But it probably would be too cold for him here, anyway."

In February, the man decided to visit his father. As luck would have it, however, his boss's wife had to have an operation, and the man had to fill in. He called his father to tell him he'd probably get to Florida in March or April.

I met the man on Friday. He had finally come to Tampa. He was here to bury his father.

I offered the man a glass of water. He cried. I put my arm around his shoulder and he collapsed, sobbing, "I should have come sooner. He shouldn't have had to die alone." We sat together until late afternoon.

That night, I asked my dad to play golf with me the next day. And before I went to bed, I told him, "I love you, Dad."

Nick Curry III, age 19

Source: From *Chicken Soup for the Teenage Soul* by Canfield, Hansen and Kirberger, Health Communications, Inc.

Comprehension: Inference and Interpretation

Complete each sentence by circling the correct letter.

1. The man's wife probably thinks _____.

a. she shouldn't have invited her father-in-law for Christmas

b. she should have invited her father-in-law for Christmas

c. she should invite her father-in-law for Christmas

2. The man probably thinks _____.

a. he should have moved to Florida

b. he should have sent his father more money

c. he should have spent more time with his father

3. Nick Curry, the author, probably thinks _____.

a. the man couldn't have done more for his father

b. the man shouldn't have done more for his father

c. the man should have done more for his father

Listening with a Purpose

Determine Context

🎧 *Listen to the conversation. Then answer each question in your own words.*

1. What is the relationship between the speakers? _____

2. What is the conversation mainly about? _____

3. Where is this conversation taking place? _____

Listening Between the Lines

🎧 *Now listen between the lines for each speaker's point of view.*
Circle the phrase that correctly completes each statement.

1. The man (is really / isn't really) sorry for what he said.

2. The man doesn't want the boy to wear an earring because he's afraid that the earring (means something important / doesn't mean anything important).

3. According to the boy, decorations (represent / don't represent) important things.

4. At the end of the conversation, the man feels that the relationship between the two speakers (is better / is worse) than before the conversation.

 **Question:** The boy says, "Dad, set your mind at ease." What do you think he means by this?

Heart to **Heart**

I'm against...   It depends.
In my opinion...
I'm for...

Talk with a partner. Is it important or necessary to apologize when you feel you have done something wrong, or is it better to express regret in some other way? Support your idea by telling about a personal experience.

I don't feel strongly about...   As far as I'm concerned...
What about you?

Vocabulary

Family Dynamics

🎧 *Say each word or phrase. Study the definitions.*

siblings: brothers and sisters

sibling rivalry: competition between children to get their parents' attention, love, or favor

an only child: a child who has no brothers or sisters

chores: small jobs that children have to do, such as washing dishes or picking up toys

an orphan: a child whose parents have died

birth parents: the biological parents of a child

adopt: become the legal parent or parents of a child with different birth parents

adoptive parents: parents who adopt a child

Read the story. Fill in each blank with the correct vocabulary item.
Use each word or phrase only once.

Happily Ever After

When Fern and Bob Franson discovered that they couldn't have children of their own,

they went to an agency to try to _____ a child. Things didn't look
_{1.}

promising at first, but eventually the agency called them to report that a little girl

named Angela was available for adoption. Soon Angela was part of their family.

All went well for about four years, until Fern and Bob decided they didn't want

Angela to be a(n) _____ and that it would be better if she had
_{2.}

a(n) _____. They went back to the agency and asked to adopt a second
_{3.}

child. This time they didn't have to wait so long. Within four months, they were the

proud _____ of Jasper, a healthy five-year-old boy. Jasper hadn't had
_{4.}

an easy or ideal life up to this point. He was a(n) _____ whose
_{5.}

_____ had died in an accident and who had lived in a government
_{6.}

home for almost three years. Fern and Bob were delighted to have another child,

however, so they excitedly took him home and introduced him to Angela. Jasper was

happy to have a sister, but Angela wasn't so happy to have a brother. Before too long a

fierce _____ developed between the two children. Suddenly Angela
_{7.}

wanted to play with toys she hadn't played with for months. Whatever Jasper had, Angela

wanted, and whatever Angela had, Jasper wanted. For more than two years, life was

difficult in the Franson family. Angela and Jasper didn't get along at all, and Angela even

started refusing to do the simplest _____, like picking up her toys.
_{8.}

Bob and Fern wondered if they should ever have adopted a second child at all. They

continued to show both children a lot of love, however, and to do a lot of things together

as a family. By the time Jasper was seven and Angela was six, things had improved greatly.

Though the two children didn't always get along, they seemed well on their way to being

happy and well adjusted.

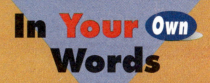

▶ **Speaking**

Warm up: Talk about the pictures with a partner. • Who are the people? • What's the problem? • How does the father try to reassure the mother?

Then: Create conversations for the people. OR Talk about the family. Say as much as you can.

▶ **Writing:** A Short Narrative

Reread the story that Nick Curry III told on page 21. Write about your reaction to the man in the story. OR Tell a true or fictional story about a conflict between family members.

25

He may have disappeared on purpose.

Warm up: *What do you like about mystery stories?*
Read or listen. 🎧

Have you heard the news?

What news?

Mel, the guy in charge of the mailroom, is missing.

TOWERS ADVERTISING

What do you mean, Mel's missing?

Well, he's disappeared. No one knows where he is.

That's unbelievable. Mel . . . ? How did you find out about this?

It's in the paper. Here. Have a look.

I must've missed it. This is awful. . . . "Mel Shaw, 53, an employee of Towers Advertising, has been missing since Friday. According to his wife, Mary, Mr. Shaw didn't return from work Friday evening."

Comprehension: Confirming Content

Mark the following statements **true, false,** *or* **I don't know,** *according to the photo story.*

	True	False	I don't know.
1. Mel is single.	☐	☐	☐
2. Mel has children.	☐	☐	☐
3. Mel works for the post office.	☐	☐	☐
4. Mel likes his job.	☐	☐	☐
5. Mel went to work Friday morning.	☐	☐	☐
6. Mel was taken to a hospital.	☐	☐	☐

Tell a partner what you know about Mel Shaw. Use your own words. Say as much as you can.

GRAMMAR AND MEANING

Must have, may have, **and** might have

Receptive Model

Listening Focus • A Conversation

Before You Listen: *When you read or hear about a mystery, do you like to guess what might have happened?*

🎧 *Listen to the conversation between two police detectives about Mel Shaw.*

Comprehension: Factual Recall

🎧 *Listen to the conversation again. Mark the following statements **true** or **false**. Make the false statements true. Then listen again to check your answers.*

		True	False
1.	The two speakers work for the police department.	☑	☐
2.	Mel was seen at a fish restaurant.	☐	☒
3.	Mr. and Mrs. Shaw are not divorced.	☒	☐
4.	The captain of the department is one of the speakers.	☐	☒
5.	Mel Shaw is not in any nearby hospital.	☒	☐
6.	The speakers don't know what happened to Mel.	☑	☐
7.	Both speakers have the same opinion.	☐	☒

Must Have, May Have, **and** Might Have

Use **must have, may have,** or **might have** + past participle to draw conclusions about the past.

Use **must have** if you are almost sure.

> **A:** Paul was coughing on Monday. And he was out on Tuesday.
>
>   *must have*   *past participle*
> **B:** He **must have caught** a cold.

Use **may have** or **might have** if you think something was possible, but you aren't sure.

> **A:** Where's Jane?
>
>   *may have*   *past participle*
> **B:** She **may have stayed** late at the office.

TIP: When you use **must, may,** or **might** to make a negative conclusion, don't contract.
     He **must not** have been happy.

GRAMMAR TASK: Find a sentence in the photo story on pages 26–27 in which a speaker draws a conclusion.

28   UNIT 3

Grammar in a Context

Complete each sentence with **must have** or **might have** and the indicated verb.

Gail: Sue? How are you? Where have you been hiding?

Sue: I haven't been hiding. I met a great guy at work.

Gail: You know, I tried calling you all last week. You _____ out every evening.
1. be

Sue: That's right!

Gail: Well, tell me all about him. What's he like?

Sue: He's very cute and intelligent and he's got great taste in music. . . . There's really only one little thing.

Gail: Oh?

Sue: He told me he'd been married, but whenever I ask about his wife, he changes the subject.

Gail: He _____ a messy divorce.
2. have

Sue: That's possible. Or his wife _____ in some terrible accident.
3. die

I'm pretty sure something awful _____.
4. happen

Gail: Give the guy the benefit of the doubt. Maybe when he's with you he just doesn't want to talk about another woman. What's his name, anyway?

Sue: Shawn Melon.

Grammar with a Partner

Partner B, turn to page 142 and read your sentences to Partner A.

Partner A, listen to Partner B's sentences. Respond with one of the conclusions in this box.

Partner A's Conclusions

1. It must have cost a fortune.

2. They might not have understood it. Or it might not have been funny.

3. She might not have received it. Or she might have been too busy to call or write.

(continued on next page)

Now, Partner A, turn to page 142 and read your sentences to Partner B.

Partner B, listen to Partner A's sentences. Respond with one of the conclusions in this box.

Partner B's Conclusions

4. She may have forgotten it.

5. She must have forgotten her keys. She may be waiting for her husband to get home.

6. She must have been driving very fast.

SOCIAL LANGUAGE 1

HOW TO speculate about possibilities

Conversation

🎧 *Read and listen to the conversation.*

A: I'm beginning to worry. Sam hasn't returned my calls.

B: How long have you been trying to reach him?

A: Well, since Tuesday.

B: He might have gone on vacation. Or he may be visiting a friend. Don't jump to conclusions so fast.

A: Yeah, you're probably right.

🎧 *Listen again and practice.*

Variations

reach him
call him
get in touch with him

Improvise

Improvise a conversation with a partner. One of you has been trying to call a mutual friend for some time without success. The other partner speculates about why no one answers. Use the conversation as a model.

Some Ideas

may be on-line

might have gone on a cruise

might have gone on a business trip

or your OWN idea

☑ **Now you know how to speculate about possibilities.**

HOW TO tell someone you took something by mistake

Conversation

🎧 *Read and listen to the conversation.*

A: I'm not sure, but I think I may have taken your umbrella by mistake. Is this yours?

B: Yes, it is. Thanks.

A: Mine looks just like it.

B: Well, you've got great taste in umbrellas.

🎧 *Listen again and practice.*

Improvise

Improvise a conversation in which you think you mistakenly took something that belongs to your partner. Or else your partner has mistakenly taken something of yours. Use the conversation as a model.

Some Ideas

jacket   hat   sunglasses   keys

gloves   watch   briefcase   purse

or your OWN idea

☑ **Now you know how to tell someone you took something by mistake.**

*Solve these riddles with a partner. Use **must have** in your answer.*
(See page 142 for answers.)

1. When George and Rachel were found, they were both dead. There was water and broken glass all around them. Why?

2. A pilot's brother died, but the man who died didn't have any brothers. How could that be?

3. When Marie was a child, she lived on the tenth floor of an apartment building. Each morning Marie rode the elevator down and walked to school.

In the afternoon, Marie took the elevator to the third floor and walked up the rest of the way. Why?

4. A man was walking down a road looking for a village called Choo, where people always told the truth. In nearby Fink, the people never told the truth. The man came to a fork in the road. One way led to Choo and the other to Fink. He didn't know which was which.

Then a woman approached. He couldn't tell whether she was from Choo or from Fink. So he asked one question. Based on the woman's answer, he took the correct road, the one that led to Choo. What must he have asked?

Receptive Model

Listening with a Purpose

Determine Context

🎧 *Listen to Part I and then complete the statement by circling the correct letter.*

This is _____.

a. a radio play   **b.** a guessing game   **c.** a detective story

Listening Between the Lines

🎧 *Now listen between the lines so you can speculate about how to complete these sentences.*

1. The mystery guest might be _____.

2. The mystery guest's father might have been _____.

Now listen to Part II. Then draw conclusions. Complete the following sentences.

1. The mystery guest must be _____ .

2. The mystery guest's father must have been _____ .

Authentic Reading
from the *Seattle Post-Intelligencer*

Before You Read: *What are some reasons why people sometimes disappear?*

Read parts of a newspaper article.

12-year memory loss called 'extraordinary'

by TOM PAULSON

If Jody Roberts forgot who she was for 12 years and simply went on to a new life with no evidence of brain damage, it's one for the medical history books, say experts in neurology and memory.

"It is extraordinary, bordering on the unique, for a case of amnesia of psychological origin to last 12 years," said Dr. Vernon Neppe, professor of neuropsychiatry at the University of Washington and director of the Pacific Neuropsychiatric Institute, a private research facility in Seattle.

A 1985 news report and police records show that Roberts was found wandering in a shopping mall in Denver just five days after she failed to show up for work at the Tacoma News Tribune. She then began a new life in Colorado.

A King County detective says he believes her story.

"I found nothing in anything that I've learned about her that leads me to doubt the validity of her story," said Tom Jensen, a King County detective.

"She was last seen May 20, and on May 25 she approached people in the mall and said she didn't know who she was. If she wanted to be lost, why go to authorities and say, 'Help me figure out who I am'?" Jensen asked.

What raises questions, however, is the fact that Roberts—prior to disappearing—had withdrawn money from her bank account and taken her pet cats to the Humane Society.

"I can't imagine that one would clear out their bank account and give away their pets in anticipation of having an episode of amnesia," said one local psychiatrist skeptical of Roberts' claim.

If this is a case of "fabricated amnesia," said Elizabeth Loftus, another professor of psychiatry, it wouldn't be quite so unusual.

"We've all heard stories about people who simply leave everything behind," said Loftus. "I'm sure there are even more people who want to do this but don't have the guts to pull it off."

Comprehension: Understanding Meaning from Context

Circle the letter of the choice that best explains the underlined word or phrase.

1. 12-year memory loss called '<u>extraordinary</u>'

   a. very dangerous   **b.** very normal   **c.** very unusual

2. Roberts was found wandering in a shopping mall in Denver just five days after she failed to <u>show up for</u> work at the Tacoma News Tribune.

   a. come to   **b.** leave   **c.** find

3. What raises questions, however, is the fact that Roberts—<u>prior to</u> disappearing—had withdrawn money from her bank account and taken her pet cats to the Humane Society.

   a. after   **b.** while   **c.** before

4. What raises questions, however, is the fact that Roberts—prior to disappearing—had <u>withdrawn money from her bank account</u> and taken her pet cats to the Humane Society.

   a. put money into her bank account   **b.** not touched her bank account   **c.** taken money out of her bank account

5. "I can't imagine that one would clear out their bank account and give away their pets in anticipation of having an episode of amnesia," said one local psychiatrist <u>skeptical of</u> Roberts' claim.

   a. who believes   **b.** who doesn't believe   **c.** who didn't hear about

Comprehension: Inference and Interpretation

Check the statements that are probably true.

_____ **1.** Dr. Vernon Neppe, professor of neuropsychiatry, thinks Jody Roberts must have been telling the truth.

_____ **2.** Detective Tom Jensen thinks Roberts must have really had amnesia.

_____ **3.** One local psychiatrist who talked about Roberts' taking her cats to the Humane Society thinks Roberts might not have really had amnesia.

_____ **4.** Professor Elizabeth Loftus thinks Roberts might have wanted to disappear.

Heart to Heart

I'm against...
It depends
In my opinion...
I'm for...

Why would someone want to disappear? What do you think might have happened in the case of Jody Roberts? Talk with a partner. Compare your opinions.

I don't feel strongly about...
As far as I'm concerned...
What about you?

Vocabulary
All About Mystery

🎧 *Look at the pictures. Say each word or phrase.*

His disappearance is **a mystery**.

A **mysterious** figure walked down a dark street.

The detective **has solved** the mystery.

This book is about an **unsolved** mystery.

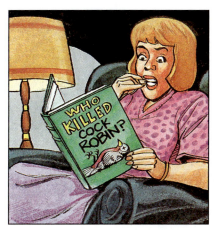

She's reading **a whodunit**.

He's **investigating** a crime.

They're **private investigators**.

The movie is **suspenseful**.

He's **puzzled**.

They've found **a clue**.

Vocabulary Practice

Look at the pictures again. Then complete each sentence by circling the correct letter.

1. A mystery is _____.

   a. something you understand and aren't curious about

   b. something impossible to ever understand

   c. something you don't understand completely but wonder about

2. A private investigator is _____ working on his or her own.

   a. a teacher

   b. a detective

   c. a scientist

3. A clue is _____ that helps solve a mystery.

   a. a thing or piece of information

   b. a person

   c. an idea

4. Something that is mysterious is _____.

   a. not important for understanding

   b. hard to understand

   c. easy to understand

5. When you investigate a situation, you _____.

   a. solve a problem

   b. spend a lot of money

   c. try to learn more about it

6. To be puzzled is to be _____.

   a. smart

   b. confused

   c. sad

7. To solve a mystery or a problem is _____.

   a. to learn more about it

   b. to find an answer to it

   c. to forget about it

8. A whodunit is _____.

   a. a plan for committing a crime

   b. a detective story about a crime

   c. a person who investigates a crime

9. An unsolved mystery _____.

   a. doesn't have an answer yet

   b. already has an answer

   c. will always have an answer

10. A suspenseful situation or story is one in which people _____ what is going to happen.

   a. don't care about

   b. are excited and nervous about

   c. are angry about

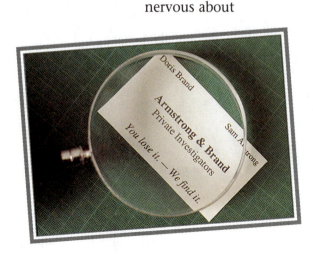

▶ **Speaking**

Warm up: Talk about the pictures with a partner. • Why is the couple talking to a private investigator in the first picture? • What was stolen? • Who might have taken it? Why?

Then: Create a conversation for the couple and the detective. OR Add details about the mystery. For example, was the clock expensive? Where would you look for clues? Why might each person have taken it? Say as much as you can.

In **Your** Own Words

LAST SATURDAY NIGHT

▶ **Writing:** A Mystery Story

Reread the photo story on pages 26–27. Then write the whole story of what might have happened to Mel. Could Mel Shaw and Shawn Melon (page 29) be the same person? Speculate and draw conclusions.

Should cloning be prohibited?

***W**arm up:* Is there a danger in changing the way new living things are created? Listen. 🎧

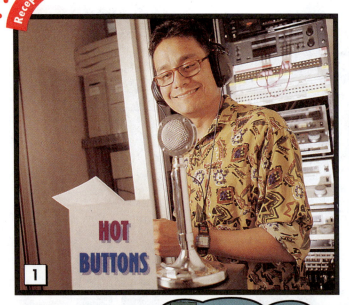

1

2

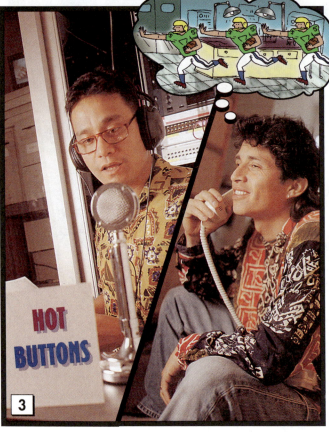

3

4

Comprehension: Understanding Meaning from Context

Circle the letter of the choice closest in meaning to the underlined word or phrase.

1. Are you for <u>cloning</u> or against it?

   a. making improved copies of living things   **b.** making positive changes in living things   **c.** making identical copies of living things

2. How do you feel about this <u>most controversial issue</u>?

   a. issue that causes disagreement   **b.** issue that all people are against   **c.** issue that people don't care about

3. But don't you think it could be <u>beneficial</u> in some ways?

   a. good   **b.** bad   **c.** interesting

4. So you think cloning <u>should be prohibited</u>?

   a. should be allowed   **b.** should not be allowed   **c.** should be increased

Tell a partner about cloning. Why are some people for it? Why are some people against it? Use your own words. Say as much as you can.

Reading Focus • A Magazine Article

Before You Read: Do you think technology can go too far?

Read the article. (Note the examples of the passive voice in bold type.) 🎧

Science Today

Genetic Engineering: Forward or Backward?

by Nanette Mikulski

One question that **is being debated** these days is whether or not genetic engineering is a good thing. Nanette Mikulski, our science editor, has contributed this article to help our readers become more informed on the issue.

We're hearing this term "genetic engineering" with increasing frequency these days. For those readers who may not be sure of its meaning, some definitions follow. When we speak of genes, we are referring to chemical substances in the cells of all living things that establish an organism's characteristics. Genetic engineering is the changing of certain genes, usually to improve an organism in some way. In recent years, for example, certain genes **have been placed** in tomato plants to make tomatoes taste better and keep them fresh in supermarkets for a longer time. Cows **have been treated** with a growth hormone that makes dairy cattle give more milk and reduces the amount of fat in the meat of beef cattle.

THESE NEW TOMATO PLANTS TASTE TERRIBLE. I CAN'T EAT 'EM.

ME NEITHER, THEY MAKE ME SICK!

These sound like positive things, don't they? After all, many people say, the technology exists to improve our lives. Why **shouldn't** this technology **be used**? Perhaps the issue isn't so simple, however. There are plenty of people around who oppose genetic engineering. Why?

Two specific objections come to mind. One is that the balance of nature **might be upset.** Suppose, for example, that scientists are able to genetically engineer certain plants so that insects will not eat them. This will protect the plants, but the insects **will be deprived** of a food supply—and other animals that depend on those insects for food will lose their food supply, too. A second objection is a moral question. Is it acceptable or right for us to change the makeup of living things?

Supporters of genetic engineering say the benefits outweigh the dangers. Look at all the improvements that **can be made** in plants raised for food, they say. Because of genetic engineering, plants **can be grown** that produce more fruits and vegetables and resist disease. In a world where more and more food **will be needed** in the future, this is a benefit.

The medical advances provided by genetic engineering, say the supporters, are even more impressive. Consider cancer, for example. If genetic engineering can provide a way to cure or prevent this disease, **shouldn't** it **be used**? And if genetic engineering **can be used** to kill the virus that causes AIDS, **shouldn't** it **be permitted**?

Opponents of genetic engineering say it **should be stopped,** or at least **limited.** Proponents of genetic engineering say it **should be promoted** and **expanded.** The debate goes on.

Comprehension: Understanding Meaning from Context

Circle the choice closest in meaning to each underlined word or phrase.

1. Cows have been treated with a growth hormone that makes dairy <u>cattle</u> give more milk and reduces the amount of fat in the meat of beef <u>cattle</u>.

   a. cows **b.** stores **c.** products

2. One objection is that the balance of nature might <u>be upset</u>.

   a. be affected in a good way **b.** be affected in a bad way **c.** not be affected at all

3. This will protect the plants, but the insects <u>will be deprived of</u> a food supply—and other animals that depend on those insects for food will lose their food supply, too.

   a. will have **b.** will want **c.** will not have

4. <u>Supporters of</u> genetic engineering say the benefits of genetic engineering outweigh the dangers.

   a. People who are neutral about **b.** People who are against **c.** People who are in favor of

5. <u>Opponents of</u> genetic engineering say it should be stopped, or at least limited.

   a. People who are in favor of **b.** People who are against **c.** People who are neutral about

The Passive Voice—Review

Notice the formation of the passive voice in a variety of tenses.

Calculators *are used* to do mathematics quickly.

A sheep *was cloned* by Scottish scientists.

A new subway *is being constructed* downtown.

The dinner *was being prepared* when the electricity went off.

The virus that causes AIDS *has been identified.*

Many people *will be cured* of their diseases.

That house *hadn't been painted* in twenty years.

Remember that the passive voice is used to place the focus of the sentence on the object rather than the subject.

The Passive Voice with Modals

Can, could, shall, should, ought to, had better, may, might, will, would, and *must* are modals. Passive sentences with modals are formed with *be* or *has / have been* + past participle.

New medicines **can be developed.**

Certain experiments **should** never **have been performed.**

GRAMMAR TASK: Read the article on pages 40–41 again. Find at least three uses of the passive voice with a modal.

Grammar in a Context

Use the passive voice to complete the following sentences.

Since the start of the twentieth century, many exciting medical advances _____. However, favorable
1. make
response to these advances _____
2. affect
by people's concerns about right and wrong. Today we find that choices
_____ in cases where there
3. must / make
really may be no right or wrong answer.

Science News Magazine wants to know your opinion. This survey _____
4. write
by Paul Reiss, our science editor, to find out your feelings about cloning. Please complete it and send your answers to:

Science News Magazine
P.O. Box 245
Long Beach, CA 90804 U.S.A.

The results _____ in our
5. will / print
next issue.

	Yes	No
• I believe animal cloning _____ . **6. should / control**	☐	☐
• I believe decisions about human cloning _____ by **7. should / make**		
a. the government.	☐	☐
b. the people directly involved.	☐	☐
c. scientists.	☐	☐
d. philosophers.	☐	☐
e. (other) _____ .	☐	☐

Grammar with a Partner

Now complete the survey above. Compare your answers with a partner's.

SOCIAL LANGUAGE 1

HOW TO **disagree politely**

Conversation

🎧 *Read and listen to the conversation.*

A: If you ask me, cloning should be banned.

B: Really? Why in the world do you think that?

A: Well, I think the bad outweighs the good.

B: Hmm. I guess that's one way to look at it.

🎧 *Listen again and practice.*

Variations

If you ask me,
Personally, I think
In my opinion,
As far as I'm concerned,

Variations

the bad outweighs the good
the disadvantages outweigh the advantages
it's wrong
the dangers outweigh the benefits

Improvise

With a partner, improvise a conversation about a controversial issue. Use the conversation as a model. Give specific reasons for your point of view.

☑ **Now you know how to disagree politely.**

Some Ideas

- cloning
- genetic engineering
- fur coats
- eating meat

or **your OWN idea**

SOCIAL LANGUAGE 2

HOW TO **express skepticism about something**

Conversation

🎧 *Read and listen to the conversation.*

A: Wouldn't it be great if AIDS could be cured?

B: You bet it would. But I wouldn't hold my breath.

A: Well, you never can tell. Who could have predicted the computer revolution?

🎧 *Listen again and practice.*

Improvise

Improvise a conversation with a partner. One of you suggests something unlikely. The other person is skeptical. Use the conversation as a model.

Some Ideas

humans could be cloned

people could travel through time

men could have babies

or **your OWN idea**

☑ **Now you know how to express skepticism about something.**

Authentic Reading
from The Associated Press

Before You Read: *Should cloning be used to protect endangered species?*

Read the article. 🎧

Chinese scientists may clone dwindling pandas

by Elaine Kurtenbach
THE ASSOCIATED PRESS

BEIJING—Frustrated by the failure of other artificial breeding techniques, Chinese scientists are considering cloning the animal that has come to symbolize endangered species everywhere—the giant panda.

Giant pandas mate only once a year, producing at most two cubs, only one of which usually survives. These reproductive habits have tried the patience of zoologists working to save the species.

These animals are native only to China, where the shrinking of their habitat and poaching have reduced their numbers to only about 1,000 in the wild.

"If we really can succeed in cloning them, then it will really work much better than the current methods in increasing their numbers," Chen Dayuan, a zoologist at the Chinese Academy of Sciences, said in a recent interview with China's state-run Central Television.

Chen did not say that cloning research had already begun, just that it might be a promising way to save the giant panda from extinction.

The announcement in February that researchers in

Scotland had succeeded in cloning an adult sheep by inserting genes from a 6-year-old ewe into unfertilized eggs drew attention to China's own research.

The Chinese Academy of Sciences banned research into the cloning of humans soon after the reports of the cloned sheep. But academy scientists have spoken out in support of cloning animals, and have announced several breakthroughs of their own, including the cloning of a cow from embryonic cells.

The proposal to clone pandas reflects the frustration of zoologists who, after decades of research, remain puzzled by many aspects of panda reproductive physiology.

"The pandas, particularly the females, don't go into heat often enough because of endocrine disturbances," Chen said.

For example, 13-year-old panda Xing Xing gave birth to three cubs, including a pair of twins who both survived. But in the past seven years, she has not borne any cubs, the television report said.

Pan Wenshi, a Beijing University professor who has spent more than 20 years studying the animals, argues that so little is known about their reproductive physiology that such research could cause the animals harm.

Source: The Associated Press.

Comprehension: Understanding Meaning from Context

Circle the letter of the choice that best explains the underlined word or phrase.

1. Chinese scientists may clone <u>dwindling</u> pandas.

   a. sick   **b.** decreasing   **c.** fertile

2. Giant pandas <u>mate</u> only once a year, producing at most two cubs.

   a. have sexual relations   **b.** clone babies   **c.** are studied

3. These reproductive habits have tried the patience of zoologists working to save <u>the species</u>.

   a. all pandas   **b.** a panda   **c.** the world

4. Chen did not say that cloning research had already begun, just that it might be a <u>promising</u> way to save the giant panda from extinction.

   a. poor   **b.** good   **c.** future

5. Chen did not say that cloning research had already begun, just that it might be a promising way to save the giant panda from <u>extinction</u>.

   a. reproducing   **b.** disappearing from the earth   **c.** beginning

Heart to Heart

I'm against...   It depends.   In my opinion...   I'm for...

Talk with three other partners. Imagine that you are a member of the Chinese Academy of Sciences. Would you argue in favor of or against cloning pandas? Why?

I don't feel strongly about...   As far as I'm concerned...   What about you?

Listening with a Purpose

Determine Context

🎧 *Listen to a debate on Jason Montoya's radio show. Then complete each statement by circling the correct letter.*

1. This debate is mainly about _____.

    a. improved farming methods   **b.** feeding the world's people   **c.** genetic engineering

2. The woman is _____ the idea.

    a. in favor of   **b.** against   **c.** neutral toward

3. The man is _____ the idea.

    a. in favor of   **b.** against   **c.** neutral toward

Focus Attention

🎧 *Read the statements in Column A. Then listen to the debate again. Complete each statement by circling the correct phrase.*

A	B
1. The woman believes that progress (can / can't) be stopped.	**a.** "What if this new type of chicken gets sick more easily?"
2. The woman believes that genetic engineering will help us to (live longer / cure diseases).	**b.** "We were born to make progress and to improve the world."
3. The man believes that changes caused by genetic engineering (will be mostly positive / might be negative).	**c.** "The end to human pain and suffering is in sight."
4. The man believes that we (will / won't) be able to manage genetic engineering.	**d.** "Suppose we engineer a new type of chicken that is bigger and has less fatty meat?"
	e. "Once this kind of thing is begun, it can't be controlled."

Listening Between the Lines

🎧 *Now listen between the lines. Match the quotation in Column B that supports each statement in Column A. You will not use all the choices in Column B.*

(reinforces the passive voice)

Which people do you think should be cloned? Form two teams.
Read the following situations, and talk about them with your team.
Develop arguments for or against the situations, and debate them in teams.

A. The Bells have been married for ten years. They are unable to have children. They would each like to be cloned so that they could have a biological son and daughter.

B. A young couple wants only male children. They don't want daughters. The father would like to be cloned.

C. A forty-five-year-old unmarried woman would like to have a daughter. She has a very good job and enough money to support herself and the child. She would like to be cloned.

D. Another forty-five-year-old woman is in the same situation. However, she is poor.

Pronunciation

The Glottal Stop

The word *uh-oh* shows a glottal stop. A glottal stop is made when the air in the throat stops completely for a moment. The sound also replaces *t* + vowel + *n*. The vowel sound disappears.

🎧 *Listen to the pronunciation of this sound in the following sentences.*

1. He shouldn't be forgo tten .

2. Where was it wri tten ?

3. Those mushrooms can't be ea ten .

4. That's a beautiful ki tten .

🎧 *Read and listen to the following sentences. Mark the glottal stop.*

1. It was gotten in advance.

2. Are you certain that he'll be chosen?

3. All the shirts will be made of cotton.

4. He can't have lost another button.

5. I love to go mountain climbing.

6. He was bitten by a dog.

🎧 *Listen again and repeat.*

Vocabulary

Scientific Research

🎧 *Say each word or phrase. Study the definitions.*

discover / a discovery: To **discover** is to find out or learn about something. What you find is a **discovery.**

invent / an invention: To **invent** is to create something new—for example, the telephone and the electric lightbulb. What you create is an **invention.**

(continued on next page)

construct / a construction: To **construct** is to build something new. The thing you build is a **construction.**

conclude / a conclusion: To **conclude** is to form an opinion about something. The opinion you form is a **conclusion.**

experiment / an experiment: To **experiment** is to try something new in order to learn more about it. What you do is an **experiment.**

hypothesize / a hypothesis: To **hypothesize** is to explain why something happens by making an educated guess. The explanation you make is a **hypothesis.**

patent / a patent: To **patent** an invention or an idea is to get legal ownership of it. The legal ownership is a **patent.**

do research / research: To **do research** is to study something carefully and completely. The activity is **research.**

analyze / an analysis: To **analyze** something is to study it in order to see how its parts work together. The study you do is an **analysis.**

Vocabulary Practice

Read the story. Circle the correct word.

Ever since Dr. Dean was a boy he has enjoyed doing scientific (**1.** patents / research). Five years ago he was in his laboratory doing some (**2.** experiments / discoveries) in electronic circuitry when he (**3.** concluded / discovered) a way to modify a camera to take photographs at great distances. He (**4.** hypothesized / constructed) that if he could simply add a locating device to a camera, he would have a "crystal ball." He did additional research and then made a complete (**5.** research / analysis). He used the results in working on his locating device and finally (**6.** patented / constructed) his "crystal ball." Of course it isn't made of crystal, and it's not shaped like a ball, but it does allow him to see anyone at any time in any place. Dr. Dean would like (**7.** to invent / to patent) his (**8.** invention / patent) someday, but he doesn't think that the government would believe that it is real. He has (**9.** experimented / concluded) that the world isn't ready for such an advanced device.

▶ **Speaking**

Warm up: Talk with a partner about these pictures. • What kind of laboratory is this? • What are the scientists doing? • What kind of protest is going on? • What does each side want?

Then: Create a conversation for the protesters. OR Talk about the clones. Say as much as you can.

▶ **Writing:** A Business Letter

Imagine you are applying to the United Nations Research Center for money to do research. In a short letter to the Center (Suite 1890, United Nations, New York, NY 10017, U.S.A.), explain your project. Begin your letter "To whom it may concern:"

I can have the floors refinished.

Warm up: *How would you change the look of your home, office, or school? Read or listen.* 🎧

Well, Ms. Hong, what kind of changes did you have in mind?

I'd like the office to be more inviting. Take these walls. All this gray is depressing.

I see. So would you like to have the walls painted white?

Maybe. Or maybe a warm color with white trim. Not that I want the office to look like a private home. But this place needs some warmth, some personality.

What kind of work do you do here, anyway?

This is an ad agency. We're the ones who come up with the ideas for ads. You might have seen some of our ads on TV.

Sounds like fun. . . . So, aside from the color change, what else would you like to have done?

Just about anything that'll get my staff to feel creative.

Creative? Hey, I'm not a psychologist. I can have the floors refinished or some carpets installed . . . maybe get some walls put up or taken down. I can't get people to be creative.

Well, I'd like to have the carpets removed and the floors refinished in the reception area. I'd really like each employee to be able to decide on the look of his or her own space.

Comprehension: Confirming Content

*Mark the following statements **true**, **false**, or **I don't know**, according to the photo story.*

	True	False	I don't know.
1. Mr. Stewart is Ms. Hong's boss.	☐	☐	☐
2. Mr. Stewart wants to do some work for Ms. Hong.	☐	☐	☐
3. Ms. Hong doesn't like white walls.	☐	☐	☐
4. Mr. Stewart is a psychologist.	☐	☐	☐
5. Ms. Hong likes Mr. Stewart.	☐	☐	☐

Review the photo story with a partner. Tell a partner what Ms. Hong wants and why. What suggestions does the man make? Use your own words. Say as much as you can.

Make, have, let, help, get, **and the passive causative**

Listening Focus • **A Conversation**

Before You Listen: *What are some things to think about before you buy a new house?*

 Listen to the conversation.

Comprehension: **Summarizing**

 Listen to the conversation again. Then summarize what you heard. Answer the following questions in paragraph form.

How did Beth feel about the house when she first saw it? How does she feel about it now? Why did she and her husband buy the house? What does her friend Andrea say about the house?

Bonus **Question:** Beth says, "I guess I've got cold feet." What does she mean by this?

Make, Have, Let, Help, and Get

The verbs **make, have,** and **let** can be followed by an object + base form of a verb. Use these verbs to talk about things that a person forces, asks, or allows someone to do.

> I **made Ken come** and **look** at the house.
>
> I'**ll have Mark give** him a call tonight.

The verb **help** can be followed by an object + base form of the verb or by an object + infinitive. The meaning is the same.

> Stan can **help you find** someone who does quality work at reasonable prices.
>
> Stan can **help you to find** someone who does quality work at reasonable prices.

The verb **get** is followed by an object + infinitive. Use this verb to talk about things that a person causes someone to do.

> Mark and I can **get Stan to recommend** a reasonable housepainter.

The Passive Causative

Use the passive causative to talk about services you arrange for someone to do for you. Use **have** or **get** + object + past participle.

> I **had the house repainted.**
>
> I'**m getting the grass cut** this afternoon.

GRAMMAR TASK: Find an example of the passive causative with **get** in the photo story on pages 50–51.

Grammar in a Context 1

Complete the sentences with the correct form of the indicated verbs.

Would you like to go out this evening?

I'd love to, but I can't. I have too much work. We're shorthanded. Three people have quit.

Why did they leave?

It's our new boss. First he _____ us _____ late
          1. get   stay

every Monday. And he wouldn't _____ us _____
                  2. let   come

in late on Tuesday. Next he _____ us _____ one
          3. make   work

Sunday a month. Then, he _____ us _____ in
          4. have   come

half an hour early twice a week. The ones who left got better

jobs, and the rest of us are looking hard.

Good luck.

Grammar in a Context 2

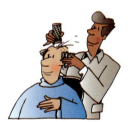

hair / dye   **hair / perm**   **ears / pierce**   **body / tattoo**   **head / shave**

*Complete the sentences. Use **have** and the correct form of the indicated verb.*

A: I could hardly recognize Bob. He's _____ his hair _____
                         1. have   dye

  green, his ear _____, and his arm _____.
              pierce   tattoo

B: What? Why in the world would he do all that? If you ask me, he

  should _____ his head _____.
       2. have   examine

A: Why? What's wrong with having a new look?

Grammar with a Partner

Read the conversation. Then use it as a model for a conversation with your partner.
Look at the pictures on page 53 for ideas.

Would you ever have your hair dyed?

Sure. That's no big deal.

Would you ever have your hair dyed green?

Now that's another story.

SOCIAL LANGUAGE 1

HOW TO state a problem/ask for a favor

Conversation

🎧 *Read and listen to the conversation.*

A: I've been having a hard time finding an apartment.

B: Hmm. I know someone who works at a real estate agency. Maybe I could get him to help you out.

A: That would be super. You wouldn't mind asking him, would you?

B: No. Not at all.

🎧 *Listen again and practice.*

Improvise

You've been having trouble doing something. Your partner knows someone who may be able to help you out. Use the conversation as a model.

Some Ideas

- getting tickets to a certain play / a theater box office
- locating a paperback copy of a certain book / a bookstore

or your OWN idea

☑ **Now you know how to state a problem and ask for a favor.**

HOW TO ask for and give advice about having something done

Conversation

🎧 *Read and listen to the conversation.*

A: My CD player isn't working.
Do you think I should <u>have it fixed</u>?

B: Maybe. How old is it?

A: About seven years old.

B: If you ask me, <u>it's not</u>
<u>worth getting it fixed.</u>

A: You think I'd be better
off buying a new one?

B: Well, you might want
to check out some
prices.

🎧 *Listen again and practice.*

Variations

have it fixed
get it fixed

Variations

it's not worth getting it fixed
it's not worth it

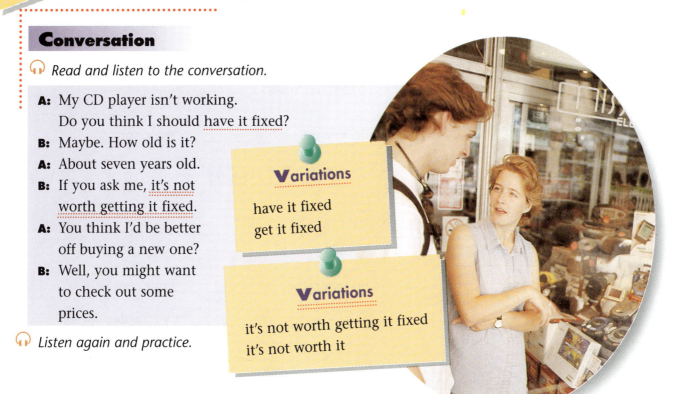

Improvise

*You are considering having something done. Your partner discusses the situation
with you and offers advice. Use the conversation as a model.*

Some Ideas

toaster / repair (fix)
VCR / repair
TV / repair

dress / take in   skirt / shorten   pants / let out

or **your OWN idea**

☑ **Now you know how to ask for and give advice about having something done.**

Inter-Action *(reinforces the passive causative)*

First fill in each blank with the indicated verb. Then answer the questions.
Break into groups and do a survey of your group. Report the results to the class.
Compare results.

Example: Two people in our group would rather buy the paper,
and three would rather have it delivered.

1. Would you rather (a) _____ the paper
<u>buy</u>

or (b) _____ it _____?
<u>deliver</u>

a. ☐   **b.** ☐

2. Would you rather (a) _____ your own hair
<u>cut</u>

or (b) _____ it _____ by a professional?
<u>cut</u>

a. ☐   **b.** ☐

3. Would you rather (a) _____ your home yourself
<u>decorate</u>

or (b) _____ it _____ by a decorator?
<u>do</u>

a. ☐   **b.** ☐

4. Would you rather (a) _____ your own cooking
<u>do</u>

or (b) _____ meals _____ for you?
<u>prepare</u>

a. ☐   **b.** ☐

Add your own question.

5. Would you rather (a) _____

or (b) _____?

a. ☐   **b.** ☐

Before You Read: *How would you make this work space more inviting?*

Read this excerpt from a business magazine. 🎧

Boxed IN

Can a round peg achieve top performance in a square hole? An office cubicle isn't the most motivating environment—but here's how to make it work.

by Nora Wood

In prison, inmates are assigned an 8-foot-by-10-foot cell; at work, employees are given a 6-foot-by-8-foot cubicle.

When Scott Fedonchik, promotions manager with *P.O.V.* magazine in New York, started his first job after college, he couldn't tell the difference between the two. Every day he would work in a tiny cubicle—number four in a row of 10. He was never exactly sure how many rows there were on his floor. Each floor in the company, which was another New York-based magazine, was exactly alike. "Sitting in that cubicle all day did feel like prison," says Fedonchik. "My creativity and morale were at an all-time low, and I think the surroundings had a lot to do with it."

Fedonchik's story is hardly unique.

After several generations of neglect, some organizations have adopted alternative office designs that promise more productive and happy employees. At *P.O.V.*, Fedonchik and his co-workers can decorate their workstations any way they like. The work environment includes a billiards table, a bar, several televisions and numerous plush couches and chairs. "This is an incredibly motivating environment. It's the type of place where you don't mind if you have to work overtime," he says.

But *P.O.V.* is the exception, with most companies sticking to the traditional office box. Working within the confines of the cubicle world, however, managers can create an environment promoting high morale and productivity without increasing costs. "The whole idea is to make employees feel comfortable. This isn't always a matter of money, it's a matter of giving them a sense of control over their environment," says Helga Wild, a research associate with the Institute for Research on Learning in Menlo Park, Calif.

The two most effective methods cited by the experts are easing restrictions on cubicle decoration and minimizing noise distractions. "They sound like little things, but these changes will work miracles with a work force," says Wild. "Letting employees create their own world in their cubicle goes a long way toward making them more productive, as well as easing the ill effects of spending most of your day in a box."

Source: "Boxed In" by Nora Wood. *Incentive,* June 1997.

Comprehension: Confirming Content

*Mark each sentence **true** or **false**, according to the reading. If the sentence is true, find the part in the reading that proves it.*

	True	False
1. Some offices are smaller than some prison cells.	☐	☐
2. When Fedonchik started his first job, he had a large office.	☐	☐
3. At *P.O.V.*, people are given a lot of choice in decorating their office space.	☐	☐
4. Many companies today have added couches, chairs, and billiard tables to their offices.	☐	☐
5. The best way to help workers feel good about their workplace is to allow them to decorate their personal space and to make certain there is not too much noise.	☐	☐

Receptive Model

Listening with a Purpose

Determine Context

🎧 *Listen to the conversation. Then answer each question in your own words.*

1. What is the relationship between the speakers? _____

2. What problem does one of the people have? _____

3. What is the person with the problem going to have to do? _____

Listening Between the Lines

🎧 *Now listen between the lines. Is George, the student with the problem, optimistic or pessimistic? Give examples of what George says to support your answer. Discuss with the class.*

Heart to Heart

I'm against...   It depends.

In my opinion...

I'm for...

Why do you think it was difficult for George to ask Jennifer for a favor? Do you ever find it difficult to ask someone for a favor? Talk with a partner. Compare your opinions.

I don't feel strongly about...   As far as I'm concerned...

What about you?

Imagine you are George. E-mail Jennifer, explaining your problem, asking for her help, and promising to do something in return. Use your own words. Say as much as you can.

Vocabulary

Services and People Who Perform Them

🎧 *Say each word or phrase. Study the definitions.*

an orthodontist: a dentist who straightens people's teeth, especially children's

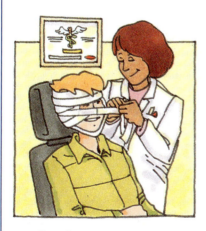

a plastic surgeon: a doctor who repairs or remodels parts of a human body

a typist: a person who types documents on a word processor

a tailor: a person who makes, fixes, and alters clothing

an interior decorator: a person who designs the appearance of the inside of a room, house, or building

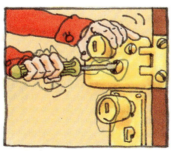

install: To **install** something is to put it in position and get it ready for use.

tune up: To **tune up** a car is to check it and adjust the brakes and the motor so that it works better.

a mechanic: a person who works in a garage, tuning up or fixing cars

a plumber: a person who installs or repairs plumbing, including sinks, pipes, and toilets

a locksmith: a person who installs or changes locks

(continued on next page)

a clinic: a place where people can go for medical or dental help

an accountant: a person who keeps financial records

Vocabulary Practice

Partner A, ask Partner B the first five questions. Partner B, answer each question.
Then, Partner B, ask Partner A the second five questions. Partner A, answer each question.

Example: **A:** Who would you go to if you wanted to have a jacket altered?
　　　　　　B: I'd go to a tailor.

Partner A's Questions

1. Who would you call if you wanted to get your car tuned up?

2. Who would you call if you wanted to have your locks changed?

3. Who would you call to get financial reports prepared for your business?

4. If you wanted to get a tattoo removed, who would you go to?

5. Who would you call if you had to get a new shower installed?

Partner B's Questions

6. If you needed to have your children's teeth straightened, who would you call?

7. Where would you go to get your blood pressure taken?

8. Who would you go to if you wanted to have a skirt or pair of pants shortened?

9. Who would you call if you wanted to have your living room redesigned?

10. Who could you contact if you wanted to get your book typed?

▶ **Speaking**

Warm up: *Talk with a partner. • What is the woman's problem with her car? • What does the man at the cleaners want done to his suit? • What do you think the women leaving the beauty salon had done to their hair?*

Then: *Create conversations for the people. OR Talk about the woman and her car or the man and his suit. Say as much as you can.*

▶ **Writing: An Essay**

Write about a person you know who inspired others to do their best. It could be a teacher, a friend, a relative, or a boss. First, introduce the person and explain how you know him or her. In another paragraph, give specific examples of how this person helped you or someone else to succeed.

Review, SelfTest, and Extra Practice

Part 1

Review

Checking In

🎧 *Listen to the conversation.*

SelfTest

Comprehension: Factual Recall

🎧 *Listen to the conversation again. Then complete each sentence by circling the correct letter.*

1. Mrs. Glisson is at the hotel _____.

   a. to relax   **b.** to attend a conference   **c.** to meet her relatives

2. Mr. Glisson and his son are at the hotel _____.

   a. to relax   **b.** to attend a conference   **c.** to meet their relatives

3. Mrs. Glisson reserved their hotel room _____.

   a. on the Internet   **b.** by phone   **c.** through a travel agent

4. The clerk couldn't find the reservation because _____.

   a. Mrs. Glisson didn't pay for the room   **b.** someone must have forgotten to enter the reservation in the computer   **c.** Mrs. Glisson never made the reservation

5. The Glissons have had a difficult day because _____.

   a. their plane had left by the time they got to the airport   **b.** they had to wait four hours for a flight   **c.** their flight was canceled

6. The son wants to _____.

   a. play volleyball   **b.** go to the gym   **c.** leave a message

Comprehension: Verb Form Review

🎧 *Listen again to the conversation. Then complete the following sentences with the correct verb forms.*

1. We _____ _____ a long, hard trip today.

2. We got into a traffic jam on the way to the airport this morning, and by the time

we _____ there our plane _____ _____.

3. I'm sure we can _____ this _____ _____. When you made the

reservation, did you get a confirmation number?

4. Whoever was on duty _____ _____ _____ to enter your reservation

in the computer.

5. You're in Room 1446. I _____ _____ the bellboy _____ your bags up.

6. No, I don't see anything from the Herzogs. They _____ not _____ _____

_____ yet.

Grammar with a Partner

The Herzogs were driving to the convention. They should have arrived before the Glissons. With a partner, speculate about why the Herzogs didn't arrive earlier.

Example: They might have stopped for something to eat along the way.

Improvise

With a partner, improvise a situation in a hotel. One person is checking in. The other person is a clerk who cannot find the reservation. Speculate about why there is no record of the reservation. Then solve the problem together.

Part 2

Review

I Think You'd Better Report This to the Supervisor.

🎧 *Read or listen.*

Well, I guess we've finished with this floor. . . . Pam, what's the matter?

SelfTest

Grammar: Past Modals

Complete the following sentences. Choose the correct modal and then write the complete verb phrase.

1. Pam _____ the camera off the dresser.
   (should / must) / knock

2. When the camera fell on the floor, the lens _____.
   (could / must) / break

3. Pam thinks she _____ so fast when she was cleaning.
   not (must / should) / work

4. The guests _____ their camera in the drawer when they went out
   (must / should) / put
instead of leaving it on the dresser.

Mark the following statements _agree_ or _disagree_.

	Agree	Disagree
1. It was Pam's fault the camera fell and broke.	☐	☐
2. Pam shouldn't have been in a hurry.	☐	☐
3. It was the guests' fault for leaving the camera lying on the dresser.	☐	☐
4. Pam could have avoided the problem.	☐	☐
5. Pam should report the situation to her supervisor.	☐	☐
6. Pam should be fired.	☐	☐

Now explain your reasons to your partner.

riting

You were a guest at a hotel when the maid accidentally dropped your camera and broke it. The hotel manager offered you an extra night at no charge. You wanted the hotel to fix or replace the camera, but the manager refused. Write a letter of complaint to the corporate offices explaining what happened and what you would like them to do.

art 3

Review

Authentic Reading

from _The Albuquerque Journal_

Before You Read: How much attention do you think children need?

Read excerpts from a newspaper article about parenting. 🎧

Children Need Attention, But Not a Lot

Parenting

JOHN ROSEMOND

More thoughts on parenthood:

To say the more attention a child gets, the better, is as ludicrous as saying the more food a child gets, the better. Children need attention, but they don't need a lot.

When they're given a steady supply of more than they need, children become dependent and begin acting like they can't get enough. Parents should have no more problem, therefore, saying "no" to a child who is making an inappropriate request for attention than they do saying "no" to a child who wants ice cream before supper.

In the last 40 years, American parents have grown increasingly dependent upon the professional "expert" to help them raise their children. In the process, they have placed themselves in grave danger of losing complete touch with their own common sense.

Parents who are constantly obsessed with making intellectually "right" decisions usually fail to do anything decisive at all.

Parents who constantly bend over backwards for their children eventually fall over backwards.

Parents who always go out of their way for their children eventually lose their way.

Parents who always put their children first may be surprised to eventually discover that their children put them last.

If you are married, the secret to successful childrearing is to pay much more attention to your marriage than you do your children.

Source: "Children Need Attention, But Not a Lot" by John Rosemond. *The Albuquerque Journal,* August 26, 1993.

SelfTest

Comprehension: Understanding Meaning from Context

Circle the letter of the choice closest in meaning to the underlined word or phrase.

1. To say the more attention a child gets, the better, is as <u>ludicrous</u> as saying the more food a child gets, the better.

   a. hard   **b.** easy   **c.** ridiculous

2. In the process, they have placed themselves in grave danger of <u>losing complete touch with</u> their own common sense.

   a. forgetting about   **b.** remembering   **c.** using

3. Parents who constantly <u>bend over backwards</u> for their children eventually fall over backwards.

   a. do nothing   **b.** do everything   **c.** do certain things

 **In Your Own Words** Read the newspaper article on page 67 again. Then tell a partner about the author's point of view.

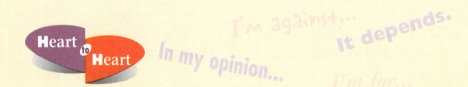 I'm against... It depends. In my opinion... I'm for...

Heart to Heart

Do you agree or disagree with the author? Has your opinion changed after reading this article? Talk with a partner.

I don't feel strongly about... As far as I'm concerned... What about you?

SOCIAL LANGUAGE Review

Review 1

🎧 *Read and listen to the conversation between Ken Herzog, Martha Glisson, and Nick Malouf.*

Ken: Martha, you see that man?

Martha: You mean the one with the beard?

Ken: Uh-huh. That's Nick Malouf, the guy who organized this conference. Let me introduce you to him.

Martha: I'd love to meet him. We've written to each other, but we've never met. I feel kind of guilty. I owe Nick an apology. I promised to try to write an article for the convention newsletter, but I never got around to it. I really should have found the time.

Ken: You've had a lot to deal with these past few months. You couldn't have done any more.

Martha: Well, maybe not. . . . Tell me, what's Nick like?

Ken: He's a really nice guy. I'm sure you'll like him.

Ken: Hi, Nick. How are you doing?

Nick: So far, so good. It's good to see you, Ken.

Ken: Good to see you, too. The program looks great. . . . Nick, I'd like you to meet my friend and colleague, Martha Glisson. Martha, this is Nick Malouf.

Martha: It's a pleasure to finally meet you in person.

Nick: It's my pleasure. I'd love to spend some time with the two of you. Maybe when things quiet down here, we can get together.

Martha: That would be great.

Improvise

You and your partner are at a conference. You introduce your partner to the person who organized the conference. Then the three of you have a conversation about the conference and the other people there.

Review 2

🎧 *Listen to the conversation between Trevor Glisson and a hotel employee.*

Improvise

Imagine you're a guest, and your partner is an employee of the hotel. Ask your partner about the pool, the exercise room, and various services of the hotel. Use the conversation as a model.

SOCIAL LANGUAGE SelfTest

Circle the appropriate statement or question to complete each of the following conversations.

1. A: Wouldn't it be great if scientists found a cure for the common cold?

    B: _____

      a. I'll bet.

      b. It's not worth it.

      c. You bet it would.

2. A: If you ask me, all cars should be banned from the center of town.

    B: _____

      a. You had a right to be upset.

      b. That's one way to look at it.

      c. I'd really like to.

3. A: _____

    B: It's a pleasure to meet you.

      a. Hey, man, here's Professor Thomas.

      b. We've met several times.

      c. I'd like to introduce you to Professor Thomas.

4. A: Do you know our new director?

    B: _____

      a. Don't let it get to you.

      b. We've met, but we're not on a first-name basis.

      c. That's a possibility.

5. A: In my opinion, high schools should be in session twelve months a year.

    B: _____

      a. You bet it would.

      b. Why in the world do you think that?

      c. I shouldn't have done it.

6. A: I shouldn't have yelled at Kathy.

B: _____

   a. I feel awful.

   b. I guess you're right.

   c. Just tell her you're sorry.

7. A: I've been having trouble with my new computer.

B: _____

   a. I'll try to get Louis to help you out. He's a whiz at computers.

   b. I'll try to help Louis. He's a whiz at computers.

   c. Louis will get you to help. He's a whiz at computers.

8. A: _____

B: If it's very old, it may not be worth it. It may cost more than a new one.

   a. I'm thinking of having my toaster fixed.

   b. Are you thinking of getting a new toaster?

   c. I'm thinking of getting a new toaster.

9. A: I think I may have taken your coat by mistake. Is this yours?

B: _____

   a. Don't jump to conclusions.

   b. You're probably right.

   c. Yes, thanks.

10. A: You wouldn't mind asking him, would you?

B: _____

   a. No. Not at all.

   b. That would be super.

   c. I've been having trouble.

11. A: _____

B: Don't let it get to you.

   a. Evan is sorry for me. I should have watched my temper with him.

   b. Evan apologized to me. I should have watched my temper with him.

   c. I really owe Evan an apology. I should have watched my temper with him.

12. A: I'm beginning to worry. Carol hasn't returned my calls.

B: _____

   a. She may go on a business trip.

   b. She should've gone on a business trip.

   c. She may have gone on a business trip.

The guy who lives next door blasts music all night long.

Warm up: *How much sleep do you need to feel well rested? Listen.* 🎧

Comprehension: Understanding Meaning from Context

Listen to the conversation again. Then circle the letter of the choice closest in meaning to each underlined sentence or phrase.

1. I hardly slept a wink.

   a. I slept for a long time.   **b.** I slept very well.   **c.** I slept very little.

2. I've tried everything in the book.

   a. to do a lot of reading   **b.** to do all that is generally suggested   **c.** to use the dictionary

3. I'm a light sleeper.

   a. I sleep with the lights on.   **b.** I sleep during the day.   **c.** Noise bothers me when I'm asleep.

4. Since then she's been sleeping like a baby.

   a. very little   **b.** well   **c.** poorly

5. It sure beats moving.

   a. It's better than moving.   **b.** It's worse than moving.   **c.** I'd really like to move.

Tell a partner about Russ's problem. Use your own words. Say as much as you can.

Reduced adjective clauses

Receptive Model

Reading Focus • A Magazine Article

Before You Read: *Do you remember your dreams?*
Read the article. (Note the examples of adjective clauses in bold type.) 🎧

The Stuff Dreams Are Made Of

by Madeleine McGowan, Ph.D.

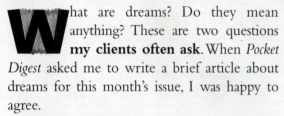

What are dreams? Do they mean anything? These are two questions **my clients often ask**. When *Pocket Digest* asked me to write a brief article about dreams for this month's issue, I was happy to agree.

So, first: What are dreams? Dreams are stories **people create, watch, and participate in while sleeping**. Dreams are imaginary, of course, but they seem real to the dreamer. Whether we are awake or asleep, our brains continually produce electrical brain waves **scientists can measure**. During sleep, there are two basic types of waves: (1) large, slow waves; and (2) smaller, faster waves. The type of sleep **that occurs when the waves are smaller and faster is called REM, which stands for Rapid Eye Movement**. Most dreaming happens during REM sleep. If you watch someone **who's asleep and dreaming**, you'll probably see that person's eyelids moving quickly. REM periods usually occur from three to five times per night. When we wake up in the morning and remember our dreams, it often seems that they've gone on for hours and hours. They haven't, though; REM periods usually last from five minutes to half an hour.

Second: Do dreams mean anything? Well, yes, they mean something. But it's a lot more difficult to assign a specific meaning to a dream than we might think. Sigmund Freud, **whose theory of psychoanalysis has dominated psychiatry in the twentieth century**, said that dreams are usually disguised wish fulfillments. Suppose, for example, you have a red-headed co-worker **you don't like who's always criticizing you**. One night you dream you're driving a car. You see a man dressed in red, and you hit him with your car. According to Freud, hitting the man in red would represent your anger at the red-haired man at work. Your dream fulfills your wish. But not all psychiatrists agree with Freud. Some say that this kind of matching of dreams and reality is too easy. The reality of people's lives, they say, is much more complex. Dreams have meanings, of course, but we shouldn't be too quick to interpret them.

Comprehension: Confirming Content

Mark the following statements **true, false,** or **I don't know,** according to the reading.

	True	False	I don't know.
1. *Pocket Digest* is a weekly magazine.	☐	☐	☐
2. Dreams are imaginary stories.	☐	☐	☐
3. In REM sleep, the electrical brain waves are large and slow.	☐	☐	☐
4. Dreams last for hours and hours.	☐	☐	☐
5. Sigmund Freud's theory of psychoanalysis is correct.	☐	☐	☐

Comprehension: Identifying the Main Idea

Which of the following statements is the main idea of the article? Circle the correct letter.

a. According to Freud, hitting the man dressed in red would represent your anger at the red-haired man at work.

b. REM periods usually occur from three to five times per night.

c. Dreams have meanings, but they aren't necessarily easy to understand.

Reduced Adjective Clauses

Remember that adjective clauses give information about nouns and pronouns.

adjective clause

The guy **who lives next door** blasts music all night long. (gives information about "the guy")

To form an adjective clause that shows possession, use **whose.**

adjective clause

You mean the woman **whose car you bought?** (= The car belonged to the woman, and you bought it from her.)

Adjective clauses begin with relative pronouns. The relative pronouns are **who, whose, whom, that,** and **which.** Relative pronouns can be subjects or objects in a clause.

    subject: Alice Fitch, **who** lives next door to me, is a sleep therapist.

    object: I have a lot of old books **that** I'd like to give away.

If the relative pronoun in an adjective clause is an object, you can drop it from the sentence.

    I have a lot of old books I'd like to give away.

Be careful! You can drop a relative pronoun only if it is an object. You cannot drop the pronoun if it is a subject.

    Alice Fitch, **who** lives next door to me, is a sleep therapist.

    (NOT ~~Alice Fitch lives next door to me is a sleep therapist.~~)

GRAMMAR TASK: Read the article on page 74 again. Find three of the sentences where the relative pronoun has been dropped. Say the sentences with the relative pronoun.

Grammar in a Context 1

Read the conversation.

Fred: How's the book going, Simon?

Simon: Done. Can you believe it? How do you like *Inside Your Dreams* as a title?

Fred: Cool.

Simon: All I have to do now is write the acknowledgments.

Fred: How many people are you going to thank?

Simon: Well, there's Dr. Smith. He gave me all the latest research on dreams.

Fred: Who else?

Simon: My editor, Erica Glass—she was fantastic. She had all sorts of ideas that helped make the book more interesting.

Fred: Anyone else?

Simon: My family, of course. I can't tell you how supportive they've been these past few years.

Fred: Is that it?

Simon: I think so.

Fred: What about your best buddy? What about me? I'm the one who told you to write the book in the first place!

Now complete the sentences in which Simon thanks Dr. Smith, Erica Glass, his family, and Fred.

1. First, I'd like to thank Dr. Smith, who _____

_____.

2. I'd also like to thank my editor, Erica Glass, whose _____

_____.

3. I want to thank my family, who _____

_____.

4. Finally, I wish to thank my friend Fred, who _____

_____.

Grammar with a Partner

*You have received a big award. Tell your partner about the people who helped you. Use **who** and **whose**. Use the conversation above as a model.*

Grammar in a Context 2

*Read these conversations. Cross out the words **who** or **that** when they are objects.*

1. A: The woman that I dreamed about had long, blond hair.

   B: What did he say?

   C: He dreamed about a woman who had long, blond hair.

2. A: The bed that I bought is very comfortable.

   B: What was that?

   C: He bought a bed that is very comfortable.

3. A: The woman who is standing over there is a famous artist.

   B: Do you mean the one who is wearing the green dress?

   C: No. He's talking about the one who is wearing a business suit.

Game *(reinforces **whose**)*

*Use **whose** to describe a classmate. The rest of the class guesses who you mean.*

Example: **A:** I'm thinking of someone whose hair is dark brown.

          B: Are you thinking of Richard?

          A: No, I'm not. I'm thinking of someone whose family name begins with a *K*.

          B: Are you thinking of Rose?

          A: No, I'm not. . . .

SOCIAL LANGUAGE 1

HOW TO make a formal complaint/ask for a refund in a store

Conversation

🎧 *Read and listen to the conversation.*

A: Excuse me.

B: Yes? How may I help you?

A: I bought this electric blanket here last week, and I'd like to return it. It doesn't work.

B: Oh. I'm sorry. Would you like to exchange it?

A: No, thank you. I'd like a refund.

B: Certainly. Do you have your sales slip?

🎧 *Listen again and practice.*

Variations

a refund
my money back
credit

Improvise

With a partner, improvise a conversation about returning something to a store and asking for a refund. Use the conversation as a model.

Some Ideas

a toaster / burns toast

a food processor / is not powerful enough

a coffee maker / leaks

"stay tuned for"

a radio / doesn't get good reception

a razor / makes too much noise

or your OWN idea

☑ **Now you know how to make a formal complaint. You also know how to ask for a refund.**

SOCIAL LANGUAGE 2
How To remind someone of a previous agreement

Conversation

🎧 *Read and listen to the conversation.*

A: John, there's something I'd like to talk to you about.

B: Uh-oh. That sounds serious. What's up?

A: It's not that serious. It's just that three weeks ago you promised to stop practicing the cello after eleven. But you haven't.

B: Gee, you're right. I forgot all about it. I'm sorry.

🎧 *Listen again and practice.*

Variations

It's just that
But
If you recall,

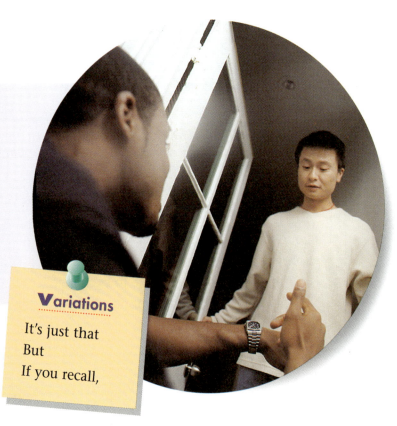

**Improvise**

Complain to your partner about something.
Your partner apologizes.
Use the conversation as a model.

Some Ideas

Your partner
- promised to stop playing the radio so loud.
- borrowed some money and hasn't paid it back.
- embarrassed you at a meeting.
- told someone a secret.

or your OWN idea

☑ **Now you know how to remind someone of a previous agreement.**

Pronunciation

Intonation to Show Interest or Lack of Interest

Our intonation can change our meaning. If we talk with no intonation (no melody), we give the listener the impression that we're not interested.

🎧 *Read and listen to this conversation.*

A: I've got a wonderful idea.

B: What?

A: I was thinking we could watch that show called "New Discoveries in Science."

B: OK.

🎧 *Now listen to the same conversation again.*

The first time, B sounded uninterested. The second time she sounded interested.

Practice the conversation with your partner.
Partner B, you may choose to sound interested or uninterested.
Partner A, how did B sound?

🎧 *Now read and listen to this conversation. Does B sound interested or uninterested?*

A: Would you like to go to that movie tonight?

B: When?

A: Eight o'clock.

B: Where?

A: At the Cineplex.

B: OK.

🎧 *Now listen to the conversation again. How does B sound this time?*

Read one of the conversations to the class. The class decides if B is interested or uninterested.

Authentic Reading

A Poem

Before You Read: *What do you think about when you walk alone in the woods or in some other beautiful place?*

Read the poem. 🎧

ROBERT FROST (1874–1963)

Stopping by Woods on a Snowy Evening

Whose woods these are I think I know.
His house is in the village though;
He will not see me stopping here
To watch his woods fill up with snow.

My little horse must think it queer
To stop without a farmhouse near
Between the woods and frozen lake
The darkest evening of the year.

He gives his harness bells a shake
To ask if there is some mistake.
The only other sound's the sweep
Of easy wind and downy flake.

The woods are lovely, dark and deep,
But I have promises to keep.
And miles to go before I sleep,
And miles to go before I sleep.

Comprehension: Understanding Meaning in Poetry

Mark the following statements **true** *or* **false,** *according to the reading.*

	True	False
1. The woods belong to the man with the horse.	☐	☐
2. The owner of the woods lives in the village.	☐	☐
3. There are other people present.	☐	☐
4. It's cold.	☐	☐
5. The man would like to stay and explore the woods, but he can't.	☐	☐

Comprehension: Inference and Interpretation

The word **sleep** *in the last two lines could mean "sleep" or something else. What do you think the word* **sleep** *could also mean? Talk with a partner.*

Do you think Robert Frost's poem is easy or hard to understand?

In your opinion, how is poetry different from other kinds of writing? Discuss your opinions with a partner.

I'm against...   It depends.

In my opinion...   I'm for...

I don't feel strongly about...   As far as I'm concerned...

What about you?

Listening with a Purpose

Determine Context

🎧 *Listen to the conversation. Then answer each question in your own words.*

1. What's the relationship between the people who are talking? _____

_____

2. Where is this conversation taking place? _____

3. Who can't sleep? _____

Listening Between the Lines

🎧 *Now listen between the lines to find the answers to these questions.*

1. What is Joe really upset about? _____

_____

2. Why does Becky suggest that Joe read the annual report? _____

_____

3. Does Becky make Joe feel better or worse about his problem? _____

_____

Vocabulary

Sleep and Dreams

🎧 *Look at the pictures. Say each word or phrase.*

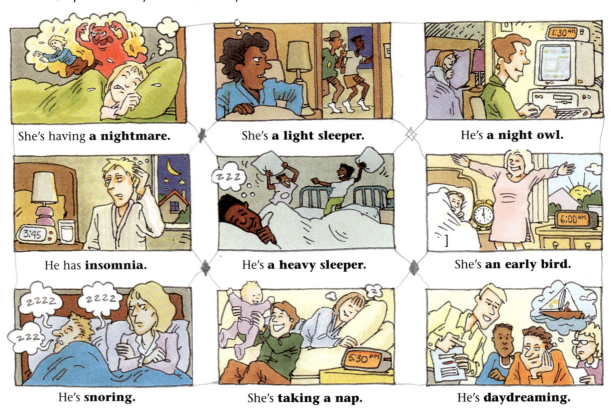

She's having **a nightmare.**

She's **a light sleeper.**

He's **a night owl.**

He has **insomnia.**

He's **a heavy sleeper.**

She's **an early bird.**

He's **snoring.**

She's **taking a nap.**

He's **daydreaming.**

Vocabulary Practice

Look at the pictures again. Fill in each blank with the correct vocabulary item. Use each word or phrase only once.

1. To breathe with a loud sound while sleeping is to ___SNORING___.

2. A person who gets up early in the morning is a(n) ___EARLY bIRD___.

3. A person who is sensitive to noise and wakes up easily is a(n) ___light sleeper___

4. A person who likes to stay up late at night is a(n) ___Night owl___.

5. A person who doesn't wake up easily is a(n) ___hEAVY sleeper___

6. To imagine something (especially a wish or hope) while awake is to ___DAY DREAMing___

7. A bad or terrifying dream is called a(n) ___NightMARE___.

8. To sleep for a short time, usually during the day, is to ___tAKing A NAP___

9. A person who often has difficulty getting to sleep may have ___iNSoMNIA___.

▶ Speaking

Warm up: Talk with a partner about the people on the plane.
• Talk about each passenger who is sleeping. • Which ones aren't? • Where do you think the plane is going?

Then: Create conversations for the man and the flight attendant, the little boy and his father, or the person with headphones and his seatmate. OR Find at least two people who are complaining and tell why. Say as much as you can.

You promised you'd read this story to me.

Dreams
by Langston Hughes

Hold fast to dreams
For when dreams die
Life is a broken-winged bird
That cannot fly.

Hold fast to dreams
For when dreams go
Life is a barren field
Frozen with snow.

▶ Writing: An Essay

Read the poem in the picture. Talk about it with a partner. Write about a dream or goal that you have. OR Make up a story that turns out to be a dream.

Unit 7

If we hadn't reached him, he would've waited forever.

Warm up: *Do you have a better memory for faces or for names?*
Read or listen. 🎧

Comprehension: Inference and Interpretation

Mark the following statements **true, false,** *or* **I don't know,** *according to the photo story.*
If a statement is false, change it to a true one.

	True	False	I don't know.
1. The people in this conversation expected heavy traffic.	☐	☐	☐
2. If the woman were in school, she'd probably have to take a lot of notes.	☐	☐	☐
3. The student who remembered every baseball statistic wasn't interested in history.	☐	☐	☐
4. School was probably difficult for Jim.	☐	☐	☐

 **Reread the photo story. Talk with a partner about different kinds of memory. Use your own words. Say as much as you can.**

The past unreal conditional

Listening Focus • A Conversation

Before You Listen: When two people see the same event, do they remember the same details?

🎧 *Listen to the conversation in a university psychology class.*

Comprehension: Identifying the Main Idea

Answer the following question.

In your opinion, why did the professor present this experiment to her class?

Comprehension: Understanding Meaning from Context

🎧 *Listen to the conversation again. Then circle the letter of the choice that best explains each sentence.*

1. If you'd told us what was going to happen, we would have paid a lot more attention to his clothes.

    a. The teacher told the class what was going to happen.

    b. The teacher might have told the class what was going to happen.

    c. The teacher didn't tell the class what was going to happen.

2. We probably wouldn't have remembered the color if he'd been wearing brown or black shoes.

    a. They didn't remember the color.

    b. They might have remembered the color.

    c. They remembered the color.

3. If he'd used a normal word like "bye" or "good-bye," we probably wouldn't have focused on it.

    a. He used a normal word.

    b. He didn't use a normal word.

    c. He might have used a normal word.

The Past Unreal Conditional

Compare these sentences.

> If I had a cell phone, I'd call him from here.

> If I had taken my cell phone, I would have called him from the beach.

The first sentence talks about an unreal condition and its result in the present. (I don't have a cell phone. I can't call from here.)

The second talks about an unreal condition and its result in the past. (I didn't take my cell phone. I couldn't call him from the beach.)

Use the past unreal conditional to talk about unreal conditions and their results in the past.

Use the past perfect form of the verb in the *if*-clause. Use **would have / could have / might have** + past participle in the result clause.

        if-clause   result clause

If you **hadn't called** me, I **would have** worried.

TIP: The result clause can be used as a statement alone.

> **A:** What would you have done if I hadn't driven by?
>
> **B:** I guess I would have waited for a police officer.

GRAMMAR TASK: Find one statement with the past unreal conditional and one with the present unreal conditional in the photo story on pages 84–85.

Grammar in a Context

Look at the cartoons. Then complete the sentences below. Use the past unreal conditional.

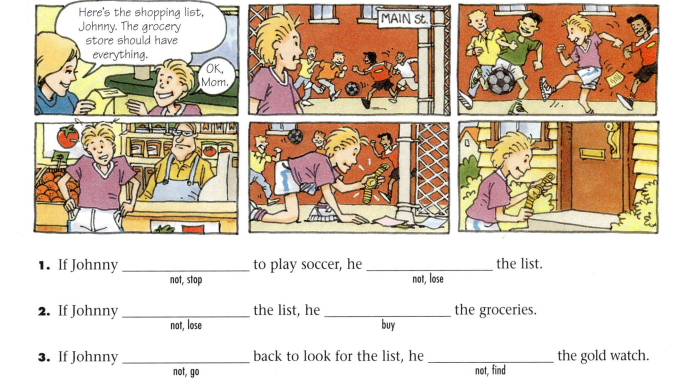

1. If Johnny _____ to play soccer, he _____ the list.
                    not, stop   *not, lose*

2. If Johnny _____ the list, he _____ the groceries.
                    not, lose   *buy*

3. If Johnny _____ back to look for the list, he _____ the gold watch.
                    not, go   *not, find*

Grammar with a Partner

The saying "Every cloud has a silver lining" means that even a bad situation can lead to something good. Think of an example from your life that demonstrates the saying. Use a past unreal conditional in your example.

Example: Several years ago I was flying to Spain for an important meeting. There was a lot of traffic going to the airport, and I missed my flight. I felt awful because I knew I would be very late for my meeting. I was late, and I lost a deal as a result. However, on the next flight I met Sarah. Since that time Sarah and I have become best friends. If I hadn't missed the flight, I wouldn't have met Sarah.

SOCIAL LANGUAGE 1

How to offer help/confirm information

Conversation

🎧 *Read and listen to the conversation.*

A: Hello?

B: Hi, Martha. Claire. How's it going?

A: Oh, I've been baking all morning.

B: Baking? If I'd known, I could've helped you.

A: You mean that?

B: Sure.

A: Well, come on over. There's plenty more to be done.

🎧 *Listen again and practice.*

Variations

You mean that?
Are you sure?
Really?
You could've?

Improvise

Tell a partner you could have or would have helped with something. Use the conversation as a model.

Some Ideas

painting

gardening

raking leaves

stuffing envelopes

or your OWN idea

☑ **Now you know how to offer help. You also know how to confirm information.**

SOCIAL LANGUAGE 2
How to request help in remembering something

Conversation

🎧 *Read and listen to the conversation.*

A: Do you have any idea what John's last name is? I'm drawing a blank.

B: Uh . . . yes. Just give me a second. It's on the tip of my tongue.

A: I think it sounds something like Linder or Linsey.

B: I've got it. It's Linsner.

A: That's it. Thanks.

🎧 *Listen again and practice.*

Variations

I'm drawing a blank.
It's slipped my mind.
I can't think of it.
I've forgotten.

Improvise

Improvise a conversation with a partner in which you and your partner try to remember something: a person's name or the name of a movie, a book, or a song. Use the conversation as a model.

☑ **Now you know how to request help in remembering something.**

SOCIAL LANGUAGE 3
How to respond to a rude question

Conversation

🎧 *Read and listen to the conversation.*

A: What did he say? What were his exact words?

B: He said, "How much did you pay for your house?" Can you believe it?

A: I would've told him to mind his own business.

B: I just said, "Why do you want to know?"

A: That's good. I'll have to remember that.

🎧 *Listen again and practice.*

Improvise a conversation with a partner. Your partner was asked a rude question. Talk about how you would have handled such a question. Use the conversation as a model.

Some Ideas

- How much do you weigh?
- How old are you?
- Who did you vote for?
- Why aren't you married?
- Why did you get divorced?

or your OWN idea

☑ **Now you know how to respond to a rude question.**

(reinforces the past unreal conditional)

When Adam Samuels died last year, he left all his money to the town he had lived in. Samuels had never married and had no relatives, but the townspeople had befriended him and taken care of him in his last years. So he asked that the money be used to help make the town a better place.

ADAM SAMUELS

Samuels had been a carpenter who built his own home. He worked hard and saved his money. He died at the age of eighty-five, leaving a fortune.

When the townspeople first heard about the money, they were delighted. But because the people couldn't decide what to do with the money, they ended up fighting over it. What could have been a wonderful gift turned out to be a nightmare.

With a partner, write as many past unreal conditional sentences as you can based on the story of Adam Samuels.

Example: If Samuels hadn't been a carpenter, he might not have built his own home.

Authentic **Reading**
from The Associated Press

***B**efore You Read: If you were learning a new skill, such as skiing, would you rather have a long lesson once a week, or a short lesson three times a week? Why?*

Read the article. 🎧

Remember this, if you want to retain what you learned.

By PAUL RECER
THE ASSOCIATED PRESS

WASHINGTON—After learning a new physical skill, such as riding a bike, it takes six hours to permanently store the memory in the brain. But interrupt the storage process by learning another new skill and that first lesson may be erased, according to research into memory and the mind.

"We've shown that time itself is a very powerful component of learning," said Dr. Henry Holcomb, a psychiatrist who heads a Johns Hopkins University group that studies how people remember.

"It is not enough to simply practice something. You have to allow time to pass for the brain to encode the new skill."

The researchers used a device that measures blood flow in the brain. They concluded it takes five to six hours for the memory of a new skill to move from a temporary storage site in the front of the brain to a permanent storage site at the back.

During those six hours, Holcomb said, there is a neural "window of vulnerability" when that new skill can be easily eroded from memory if the person attempts to learn a second new skill.

"If you were performing a piano piece for the first time and then immediately started practicing something else, then that will cause problems in retention of the initial piece that you practiced," Holcomb said.

It would be better, he said, if the first practice session were followed by five to six hours of routine activity that required no new learning.

A report on the study is to be published today in the journal Science.

"This is a new and important insight into the relationship between motor skill learning and neural activity," said Dr. Carolyn Cave, a psychologist and learning researcher at Vanderbilt University.

She cautioned, however, that not enough is known to identify precisely how the successive learning of different skills could interfere with each other.

"The brain is incredibly flexible," Cave said. "It may not be, for instance, that practicing the piano would interfere with what you learned just before from a tennis lesson. The two skills could use different parts of the brain."

Some of the Hopkins test subjects were trained in a new motor task immediately after learning the first skill. Later, those subjects were tested on how much of the first lesson they remembered, but they had lost much of the skill they had learned first.

Source: The Associated Press.

Comprehension: Factual Recall

Circle the letter of the choice that best completes each statement.

1. According to the article, a new skill is permanently stored in the brain _____.

   a. while we are learning it
   b. a short time after we learn it
   c. several hours after we learn it

2. According to the article, if you learn two new piano pieces one right after the other, _____.

   a. you will probably not remember the first one very well
   b. you will probably remember both of them equally well
   c. you will probably remember the first one but not the second one

3. According to Dr. Carolyn Cave, if you learn two different skills one right after the other, such as playing a piece on the piano and playing tennis, they _____.

   a. will interfere with each other
   b. might not interfere with each other
   c. will not interfere with each other

Comprehension: Inference and Interpretation

Imagine that a friend of yours is beginning to study two new languages at the same time. What would you recommend so that your friend could learn the languages as well as possible?

Receptive Model

Listening with a Purpose

Focus Attention

🎧 *Read the following questions. Then listen to the two conversations about memories and how they differ.*

1. Which details do the mother and father agree on?

2. Which details do they disagree on?

🎧 *Now listen again for the answers to the questions.*

Listening Between the Lines

🎧 *Now listen between the lines to help you answer the following questions.*

1. Whose memory do you think is more accurate, the mother's or the father's?

2. Do you think the mother and father have a good relationship?

Selective memory is choosing the way we remember things.
It is not necessarily remembering the way things actually were.
Explain to a partner your answers in Listening Between the Lines
on page 92.

Vocabulary

Memory

🎧 *Say each word or phrase. Study the definitions.*

recall: To recall something is to remember it.

> The old man sat on his porch, **recalling** better days.

absent-minded: Absent-minded people are forgetful about ordinary things, often because they are thinking about important questions.

> The director is **absent-minded.** She can never remember where she put her keys.

by heart: To learn something by heart is to memorize it.

> Eva is a good speller because she learned to spell a lot of words **by heart** in elementary school.

on the tip of your tongue: Something is on the tip of your tongue if you can almost but not quite remember it.

> What's that woman's name? It's **on the tip of my tongue.**

my mind went blank: When your mind goes blank, you forget something for a short period of time.

> I was so nervous at the interview that when the manager asked me my phone number, **my mind went blank,** and I couldn't answer.

by association: To learn something by association is to connect it in your mind with something easy to remember.

> I always learn names **by association.** For example, I can remember Mr. Whiting's name because he has white hair.

memorable: Something that is memorable makes a strong impression on you.

> The movie *The Sound of Music* has a lot of **memorable** songs.

a souvenir: A souvenir is an object associated with a certain place or experience. It helps to keep the memory alive.

> When we spent our summer at the beach, we brought back some seashells as **souvenirs.**

Vocabulary Practice

Complete the letter. Fill in each blank
with the correct vocabulary item. Use
each word or phrase only once.

Dear Ted,

Things are going fine here in Paris. I was having trouble learning
all the French names for the products, but some of my co-workers sat
down and helped me, and now I know them _by HEART_. I needed
to do something because _MY MIND WENT BLANK_ when I was with a
1.
2.
client the other day, and I almost lost a sale.

I really like all my co-workers. The boss is a nice guy, too, but
I'm not sure he really knows who I am. He's so _Absent-MiNDeD_
3.
that he probably doesn't remember that I'm the product manager from
Ithaca.

You remember how much trouble I have with people's names? Well,
the other day when I got to work, I ran into Bill Blake. Remember
him—blond hair, very tall and athletic? He used to work in the New
York office. He's been transferred to Paris too, but I didn't know
that. I was about to say hi, but then I couldn't remember his name.
It was _on the Tip of my Tongue_ but I just couldn't _RECALL_
4.
5.
it. Later in the day I decided I had to do something about not being
able to remember names, so I sat down and figured out how I could
remember them _by ASSOCIATION_. In Bill's case, I associated
6.
"Bill" and "Blake" with "blond." Pretty neat, eh?

Last weekend my roommate and I took a trip to Nice. We drove
along the Riviera. Beautiful place. It was really a _MEMORABLE_
7.
trip. I want to go back in the summer when it's warm enough to swim.

Not much else is new. When I come back home for the holidays,
I'll bring you some _SOUVENIRS_ from Paris. Write soon.
8.

Regards,

Ginger

▶ Speaking

Warm up: *Talk about the pictures with a partner.* • *Where are the people?* • *What are the people near the CD player trying to recall?* • *What question is the woman asking?* • *What does the woman in the red sweater think about this question?*

Then: *Create conversations for the people. OR Talk about one of them. Say as much as you can.*

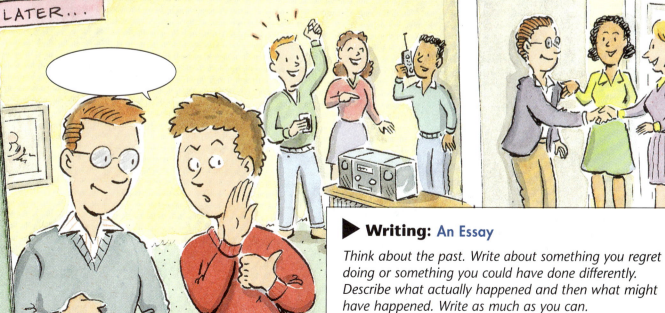

▶ Writing: An Essay

Think about the past. Write about something you regret doing or something you could have done differently. Describe what actually happened and then what might have happened. Write as much as you can.

Unit 8

You won't die if you look at some paintings.

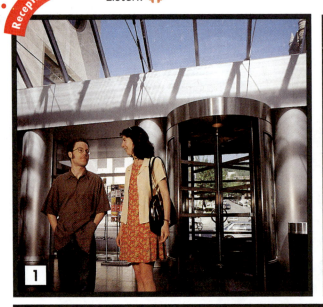

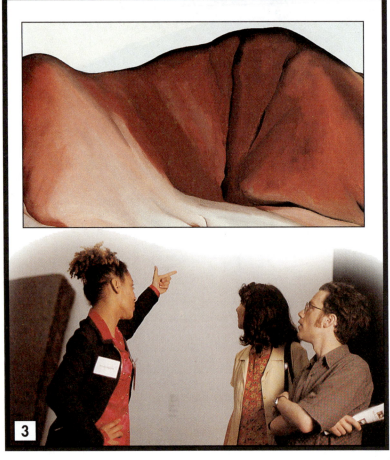

Warm up: *Do you enjoy visiting art museums? Listen.* 🎧

Receptive Model

In Your Own Words

Look at the photo story again. Tell a partner about the man and the woman and their trip to the museum. Use your own words. Say as much as you can.

Heart to Heart

I'm against...

It depends.

In my opinion...

I'm for...

Look at the three Georgia O'Keeffe paintings in the photo story. Do you like them? Why or why not? Do you consider them art? Compare opinions with a partner.

I don't feel strongly about...

As far as I'm concerned...

What about you?

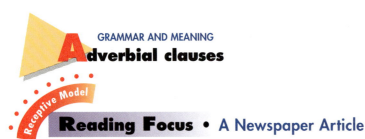

Reading Focus • A Newspaper Article

Before You Read: *Why do some people* <u>not</u> *enjoy art museums?*

Read the article. (Note the examples of adverbial clauses in bold type.) 🎧

Editor's note: In connection with next week's opening of the new downtown art museum, we asked Stanford Billings, our art critic, to provide some tips on how to get the most out of a museum trip. His comments follow.

I Don't Know Much About Art, But I Know What I Like

by Stanford Billings

Does this sound familiar? You're out with some friends and you're trying to decide what to do **when someone suggests the art museum.** You say something like, "Yuck. I'd rather go to the dentist than go to an art museum." Your friends are surprised, so you tell them, "Well, I don't understand modern art. **Whenever I go to an art museum or have a conversation about a painting,** there's always someone who tells me what I should like. And **if I don't like it**, that makes me feel there's something wrong with me. I actually do like some paintings, but I don't like being told how to react. I don't know much about art, but I know what I like."

Your reaction is not so unusual. A lot of people these days claim not to like art **because they don't understand it.** Others object to being pressured to like a painting or piece of sculpture **because it's famous.** Now the new downtown art museum is set to open next week. **If someone insists on dragging you to it,** don't despair; things are not as bleak as they seem. You can make it through the experience, and you might even get something out of it. Let me give you some tips on how to survive a visit to an art museum.

Here's the first tip: Take it easy. Go for a relatively short time and only look at a few pictures. **If you try to see everything,** you'll end up suffering from sensory overload. There's only so much your brain can absorb at one time. Don't feel that you have to get your money's worth and stay **until the museum closes.**

Second tip: Walk around by yourself, not with a spouse, a child, a friend, or a group of people. Take your time, not someone else's. You won't get much out of a piece of art **unless you experience it in your own way.** That won't happen **if you're on a schedule** or **if someone is trying to move you along.**

Third, and most importantly: Don't make a trip to an art museum an intellectual experience. Make it a personal experience. **When you walk into a room of art objects,** your eye will be attracted by certain paintings or sculptures. Go and look at those first. Be honest about your reactions. Don't try to like something just **because someone else thinks you should.** There are plenty of people who don't think much of the Mona Lisa **even though it's one of the most famous paintings in the world.** Keep this firmly in mind: **Although many works of art are world-renowned** (and therefore supposedly "good"), there's no accounting for taste.

A piece of art should be like a favorite piece of music, an exciting movie, or a fascinating book. It should speak to us personally. We need to make it our own.

Comprehension: Understanding Meaning from Context

Circle the choice closest in meaning to each underlined word or phrase.

1. Don't despair; things are not as <u>bleak</u> as they seem.

    a. surprising   **b.** expensive   **c.** depressing

2. If you try to see everything, <u>you'll end up suffering from sensory overload</u>.

    a. there will be too many things on your mind at one time   **b.** it will take too long   **c.** there will be too many people in the museum for you to enjoy yourself

3. Although many works of art are <u>world-renowned</u>, there's no accounting for taste.

    a. very expensive   **b.** very famous   **c.** very good

The author makes three suggestions about how to survive a visit to an art museum. Explain them to a partner. Use your own words. Say as much as you can.

Adverbial Clauses

The following sentence contains two parts.

          adverbial clause   *independent clause*

After Sonia finishes work, she'll buy a newspaper.

Adverbial clauses offer information about "when," "where," "how," "why," and "under what conditions" something happens, happened, or will happen. In the sentence above, the adverbial clause tells us **when** Sonia will buy a newspaper.

Be careful! When an adverbial clause refers to a future time, use the simple present tense in the adverbial clause. Use a future form in the independent clause.

     simple present tense   *future*

When I get there, I'll call him.

The following words introduce adverbial clauses.

If and ***unless*** tell us "under what conditions" something happens, happened, or will happen.

         He doesn't work ***unless he gets paid in advance.***

         If I had seen him, I would have told him.

Because and ***since*** tell us "why."

         Since we had free time, we went shopping.

When, whenever, before, after, and ***until*** tell us "when."

         They won't move ***until they find the perfect home.***

Although, though, and ***even though*** present a contrast to the idea in the independent clause.

         Although he doesn't usually go to museums, he went to one last Saturday.

GRAMMAR TASK: Find two sentences with adverbial clauses in the Reading Focus on page 98. One sentence should have the adverbial clause first. The other sentence should have the independent clause first. What is the difference in punctuation?

Grammar in a Context 1

Rewrite these sentences. Replace the underlined words with words from the box.

until	when	although	since

1. <u>Even though</u> he worked hard, they gave him a big raise.

2. Don't wait up <u>if</u> I come home.

3. <u>Unless</u> I get home, I'll work on my painting.

4. <u>Since</u> Picasso lived most of his life in France, he was born in Spain.

Grammar in a Context 2

Read each pair of sentences. Use adverbial clauses and the indicated words to connect the ideas.

Example: I won't go to sleep. I will finish my report. (until)

I won't go to sleep until I finish my report.

1. I will wait up. He gets home. (until)

2. Julie went to the Picasso exhibit. She is making a film about Picasso. (because)

3. I won't buy the painting. It is under $400.00. (unless)

4. I go to the museum. I try to take a tour. (whenever)

5. The artist continues to paint. He's a millionaire. (although)

SOCIAL LANGUAGE 1

HOW TO **explain what you like about something**

Conversation

🎧 *Read and listen to the conversation.*

A: What do you think of this one?

B: It's interesting. <u>What I like most</u> is the color.

A: I agree. I really like the way the artist uses light. I wonder if it's for sale.

🎧 *Listen again and practice.*

Variations

What I like most
What's really great
What really grabs me

☑ **Now you know how to explain what you like about something.**

HOW TO explain what you don't like about something/ acknowledge another point of view

Conversation

🎧 *Read and listen to the conversation.*

A: I can't stand this sculpture.

B: How come?

A: Well, what bothers me the most is the subject matter. It's just plain depressing.

B: Hmm. I kind of like it, but I can see what you mean about it being depressing.

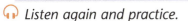

Variations

what bothers me the most
what I don't like
what turns me off
what I hate

🎧 *Listen again and practice.*

☑ **Now you know how to explain what you don't like about something. You also know how to acknowledge another point of view.**

Improvise

Improvise a conversation with a partner. Tell what you like or don't like about each of the following paintings. Talk about the subject matter, color contrast, composition, and emotional impact. Use the conversations and the photo story on pages 96–97 as models.

WYETH, Andrew. *Christina's World.* (1948).

DALI, Salvador. *The Persistence of Memory (Persistance de la mémoire).* 1931.

Masonobu. *Wandering Minstrels.* Spaulding Collection. Courtesy, Museum of Fine Arts, Boston.

HOW TO **arrange a meeting place**

Conversation

🎧 *Read and listen to the conversation.*

A: So. Are we all set for Saturday?

B: Uh-huh. I told everyone we'd meet in front of the museum unless it rains.

A: And if it rains, we'll meet inside at the information desk, right?

B: That's right. See you Saturday at noon.

A: Super. I can't wait. It should be fun.

🎧 *Listen again and practice.*

Improvise

Improvise a conversation with a partner. Set up a meeting with a group of friends at a certain time and place. Also set up an alternative meeting place if the weather doesn't allow you to meet at the first place. Use the conversation as a model.

☑ **Now you know how to arrange a meeting place.**

Inter-Action *(reinforces adverbial clauses)*

Partner B, turn to page 143.
Partner A, read the beginning of each of these proverbs to Partner B.
Partner B, read the matching ending.

a. Don't count your chickens _____.

b. Although every man knows he must die, _____.

c. Unless the job means more than the pay, _____.

Partner A, now listen as Partner B reads the beginning of three proverbs. Read the matching endings to Partner B.

d. _____, even when he tells the truth.

e. _____, they are worth knowing well.

f. _____, they remember how well you did it.

Authentic Reading
from *Living with Art*

Before You Read: *In what ways do you think artists differ from other people?*

Looking at children's art supports the conclusion that there is an inborn human desire to create and enjoy art. In this essay you will read about one child's growing power of expression.

Read the essay. 🎧

Children's Art

All of us begin to play with art as children, but in our teens most of us turn away from that kind of free expression in order to concentrate on learning the numerous rules of success in our complicated society. By looking at children's art we can get some idea of how an individual's power of expression grows. The book *Heidi's Horse* follows the progress of one child, Heidi Scheuber, from age two to age nine.

At two Heidi began with random scribbling that expressed her joy in making marks. At three she made organized circular swirls, and at four separate shapes and shapes within shapes. At four years and three months human and animal figures appeared, made of circles and straight lines. A few months later Heidi produced a horse composed of the same elements. Heidi's progress reflects the normal pattern of human development, from formless marks to forms with meaning. This gradual expansion of form and meaning is the story of art, both for the individual artist and for civilization as a whole.

Heidi's drawings of horses when she was between five and nine years old show the burst of creative development we all go through at that age. This urge, however, often is lost between age nine and the teens. The creative freedom of the younger child is overwhelmed by the desire, experienced by most older children, for realism and accuracy. Awareness of the world has expanded tremendously, and the set of marks that once seemed so satisfactory is suddenly inadequate. At this stage many children become so critical of their own efforts that they give up and never draw again. The ones who don't give up, who persevere and retain their ability to play freely with forms, become the people we call "artists."

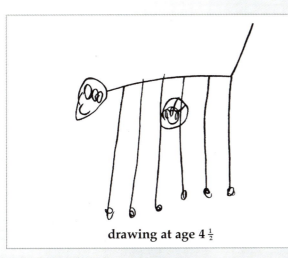

drawing at age 4½

drawing at age 5

(continued on next page)

We might speculate that there is something of the child in all artists—not in the sense of immaturity or lack of intellectual development, but in the ability to experiment, uncensored by conventional standards of good and bad. Pablo Picasso was an immensely sophisticated artist, and certainly he knew that what he made was called art—by himself and by the world. Yet throughout his life he retained this ability to play, even to "draw" joyfully in the air with a flashlight. Could it be that the artist lives in all of us until and unless something destroys it?

drawing at age 6

Source: *From Living with Art, Second Edition* by Gilbert and McCarter. Copyright © 1985, 1988, Alfred A Knopf Inc.

Comprehension: Understanding the Main Idea

Circle the letter of the idea that is not expressed in the reading.

a. Since most artists are like children, they enjoy life more than other people.

b. At a certain age, most children stop drawing because they aren't satisfied with their results.

c. Although society may expect certain things, artists are not afraid to do things in a different way.

Pronunciation

Rhythm and Intonation

In speaking and in reading aloud, speakers usually pause at the end of a "thought group," a group of words that expresses a thought. One kind of thought group is a clause. Listen to this sentence with two clauses from the Reading Focus on page 98. 🎧

I don't know much about art, but I know what I like.

Notice that the speaker pauses at the end of the first thought group and then pauses again at the end of the second thought group, the end of the sentence.

🎧 *Read and listen again to the Reading Focus. Then choose sentences in the last paragraph that have more than one thought group. Mark the places where the speaker pauses to indicate a thought group. Then practice reading the sentences with a partner.*

Now do a class reading of the entire Reading Focus. Each student reads one sentence and tries to make it sound the way the speaker does.

Listening with a Purpose

Focus Attention

🎧 *Listen to the two conversations between Ella and her parents. Then listen again for information about Ella's career plans and choices.*

1. When Ella was a little girl, what did she decide she wanted to be?

_____

2. What is Ella doing now that she is an adult?

_____

3. What occupation did Ella's parents expect her to have?

_____

4. What has Ella decided she wants to be?

_____

Listening Between the Lines

🎧 *Now listen between the lines for each speaker's point of view. Then mark the following statements **true** or **false**. Explain the reasons for your answers to a partner.*

	True	False
1. Ella's mother likes Ella's plan more than her father does.	☐	☐
2. Ella's mother is more practical than her father is.	☐	☐
3. Ella thinks money is the most important thing in life.	☐	☐
4. Ella's father is angry at her.	☐	☐

Vocabulary
The Importance of Art

🎧 *Look at the pictures. Say each word or phrase.*

This artist is **a sculptor.**

This is some of her **sculpture.**

The painting is on **an easel.**

(continued on next page)

This artist is doing **a sketch**.

This is an **abstract** painting.

This woman is **a model**.

Fruit is **the subject** of his sketch.

This painting is **a landscape**.

This painting is **a still life**.

He's painting her **portrait**.

Vocabulary Practice

Match each term in Column A with its definition in Column B.

Column A

1. a sculptor

2. sculpture

3. a sketch

4. an easel

5. a portrait

6. a landscape

7. abstract

8. a still life

9. the subject

10. a model

Column B

a. a person that an artist paints

b. a drawing usually done quickly and not very completely

c. a work of art that shows a nonliving object such as fruit

d. an artist who makes art from stone, metal, wood, or other materials

e. the main thing that a painting is about

f. works of art such as statues made of stone, metal, or wood

g. a painting of a person, especially the person's face

h. a painting of scenery

i. a work of art that is not realistic

j. a structure that holds a painter's work

▶ Speaking

Warm up: *Talk about the artwork with a partner.* • *What kinds of art does this museum exhibit?* • *What are different people doing in the museum?* • *What opinions do different people have about the abstract painting?*

Then: *Create conversations for the people. OR Talk about one of the paintings. Use **although, unless, because, until,** and **when**. Say as much as you can.*

▶ Writing: An Essay

Write about a painting that you know and like. Describe the painting so that the reader has a clear picture of it. If you can, write about the artist. Tell the reader why you like the painting and how it makes you feel. Write at least two paragraphs.

107

Unit 9

He said he'd missed his train.

Warm up: What advice would you give someone who is going to a job interview? Read or listen. 🎧

So Tim, what was your impression of the guy you interviewed this morning?

The one who used to work for Pantel?

Uh-huh.

Good. Very well informed. And he asked some great questions. The only problem was he was supposed to be here at ten and . . .

When did he show up?

Twenty after.

What was his excuse?

He said he'd missed his train. Pretty lame. . . . I was about to ask him more, but he quickly changed the subject.

Maybe we should consider the guy we interviewed yesterday.

The red-haired guy?

That's the one. I liked him. He seemed like a hard worker and a real company man. Also, he had a fantastic resume—lots of experience . . . and degrees from top schools.

I know. There was just one thing he said that raised a red flag for me.

Oh? What was that?

Remember when you asked him what changes he would make to our distribution system?

Yes.

He said he'd do whatever we told him. For a job at that level we need someone with ideas and leadership ability, not someone who just follows orders.

That's a good point.

Comprehension: Understanding Meaning from Context

Read the photo story again. In the photo story, find another way to say the following underlined sentences or phrases.

1. <u>What did you think of</u> that man?

_____

2. His excuse was <u>not convincing</u>.

_____

3. <u>His summary of his work experience was excellent.</u>

_____

4. That <u>made me think there could be a problem</u>.

_____

 **The people in the photo story interviewed two job candidates. With a partner, discuss their impressions of the two men. Use your own words. Say as much as you can.**

Quoted and reported speech and **be supposed to**

Listening **F**ocus • A Conversation

B*efore You Listen:* What do you think a job candidate shouldn't do in an interview?

🎧 *Listen to the conversation about a job interview.*

Comprehension: Understanding Meaning from Context

🎧 *Listen to the conversation again. Then circle the letter of the choice that best explains each underlined sentence or phrase.*

1. The interview was supposed to start at ten.

    a. It started at ten.   **b.** It didn't start at ten.

2. I said I'd missed the train.

    a. I told him. Then I missed the train.   **b.** I missed the train. Then I told him.

3. They said my qualifications were really good and they'd be in touch.

    a. They would be in touch in the future.   **b.** They had been in touch in the past.

4. You know you're always supposed to write a short thank-you note after an interview?

    a. it's possible to write a thank-you note after an interview   **b.** it's a good idea to write a thank-you note after an interview

Comprehension: Inference and Interpretation

🎧 *Listen to the conversation again. Then answer the following questions in your own words.*

1. Why was the husband upset after his interview?

2. What did his wife tell him to include in a thank-you note? Why?

Quoted Speech and Reported Speech

This is how we quote or report the speech of another person.
    Sam said, "I want that job." (quoted speech)
    Sam said he wanted that job. (reported speech)

In quoted speech, use quotation marks to enclose a speaker's actual words. Note the comma after the reporting verb ***said.***

Use ***tell*** (+ person) when you want to include who heard the speech.
    Sam told his wife, "I want that job."
    Sam told his wife he wanted that job.

Use ***say*** when you want to focus on the speech and not on who heard it.
    Helen said, "I can't come to the party."
    Helen said she couldn't come to the party.

Verb Changes in Reported Speech

The verb changes in reported speech in several ways. Here are some examples.

Quoted speech	Reported speech
Sam said, "I **want** that job."	Sam said he **wanted** that job.
Lenore said, "I**'m working.**"	Lenore said she **was working.**
Melanie said, "I **haven't been** there."	Melanie said she **hadn't been** there.
Arthur said, "I**'ll be** there."	Arthur said he **would be** there.
Ben said, "I **went** to the movies."	Ben said he **had gone** to the movies.

TIP: In speech and informal writing, the past is sometimes used instead of the past perfect. Ben said he **had gone** to the movies *or* Ben said he **went** to the movies.

Notice what happens when we report a **yes-no** question.

"Marty, do you want to go to the movies?" Alice asked.

Alice asked Marty if he wanted to go to the movies.

GRAMMAR TASK: Find two sentences in reported speech in the photo story on pages 108-109. Rewrite them as quoted speech.

Marty, do you want to go to the movies?

I asked Marty if he wanted to go to the movies.

Grammar in a Context

David and Marco are co-workers.
Read their telephone conversation.

Marco: Hello?

David: Hi, Marco? David.

Marco: Hi, David.

David: Is everything OK in São Paulo?

Marco: Yes. Things are going fine here.

David: Listen, we still haven't received your report. Is it ready?

Marco: Yes, it is. I just want to look it over and then I'll fax it right out. Let me know if it's OK.

David: Great. I'll see you at the conference in Bogotá next week, right?

Marco: I'll be there Tuesday evening.

David: Have you met the new Latin American marketing manager?

Marco: No, not yet.

David: Well, when you do, let me know what you think of her.

Now David's boss is asking David about Marco. Look back at the conversation on page 111. Then complete each sentence with the indicated verb.

Boss: So you spoke to Marco. What did he say? How are things in São Paulo?

David: He said things _____ fine there.
$\qquad$ **1. go**

Boss: Has he finished the report?

David: He said he just _____ to look it over and then he _____ it to us.
$\qquad$ **2. want** $\qquad\qquad\qquad\qquad$ **3. fax**

Boss: And what about the conference? Will he be able to get there?

David: He said he _____ there Tuesday evening.
$\qquad$ **4. be**

Boss: Did he have anything to say about the new marketing manager?

David: He said he _____ her yet.
$\qquad$ **5. not, meet**

Be Supposed To

Be supposed to expresses strong expectation. It is followed by a base form.

be supposed to   base form

It**'s supposed to rain** today. (The weather channel says it will rain today, but it may or may not.)

Drivers **are supposed to signal** before turning. (They're expected to do that, though many of them don't always.)

Be supposed to is used only in the present and past.

When ***be supposed to*** is used in the past, it suggests an action that didn't happen.

Bill **was supposed to** call me. (Suggests that he didn't call.)

When ***be supposed to*** is used negatively in the past, it suggests an action that did happen.

You **weren't supposed to** tell them. (Suggests that you did tell them.)

GRAMMAR TASK: Find the sentence with ***be supposed to*** in the photo story on pages 108–109. In your own words, explain what it means.

Grammar in a Context

*Complete the conversation with **be supposed to** and the indicated verbs.*

Sally: Hello?

Mom: Hi, Sally.

Sally: Oh, hi, Mom.

Mom: Sally, Dad and I would like to meet you at the airport. What time _____ your plane _____?
    1. arrive

Sally: Two-thirty. But you'd better check with the airline before you leave home.

(Later)

Dad: OK, hon. Are you ready to go?

Mom: Yes, but there's been a delay. The plane _____ Mexico City at two-thirty,
    2. leave
but it didn't. Now they've rescheduled it, and it _____ here at four.
    3. get
We don't have to leave yet.

SOCIAL LANGUAGE 1

HOW TO express uncertainty about an event's outcome/offer support

Conversation

🎧 *Read and listen to the conversation.*

A: How did the meeting go?

B: I think it went well, all in all. But it's hard to tell.

A: Is there anything I can do to help at this point?

B: No, not really. But if I do think of something, I'll let you know.

A: Well, feel free to call on me anytime.

Variations

all in all
on the whole
considering
overall

🎧 *Listen again and practice.*

☑ **Now you know how to express uncertainty about an event's outcome. You also know how to offer support.**

HOW TO **express confidence/congratulate someone**

Conversation

🎧 *Read and listen to the conversation.*

A: How did your interview go this morning?

B: Super.

A: So you're pretty sure it's going to work out?

B: Well, not absolutely positive. But it looks very good.

A: Well then, congratulations and good luck.

🎧 *Listen again and practice.*

☑ **Now you know how to express confidence. You also know how to congratulate someone.**

Variations

Super.
Great.
Piece of cake.
Fantastic.

Improvise

Ask a partner about a recent event. Your partner tells you how it went, and you respond. Use the conversations as models but add information.

Some Ideas

a business meeting

a doctor's appointment

a tryout for a play

or your OWN idea

Authentic Reading

from *The New York Times*

Before You Read: *If you wanted to hire someone to work at your fast-food restaurant, what kinds of questions would you ask?*

The following chart and reading passage are taken from an article about psychological tests for job applicants.

Read the article. 🎧

Trying to Get a Job? Check Yes or No

Tests Are Becoming Common in Hiring

By CONSTANCE L. HAYS

Do you see yourself performing in a Vegas nightclub act?

Would you rather meet people or read a book?

Does driving give you a feeling of power?

These are not queries from the local tarot-card reader, but the kinds of questions job applicants nationwide increasingly face in the process of being hired. Companies large and small are turning to psychological tests, developed by a virtually unregulated test-publishing industry, to try to determine who is too impulsive, who falls short in the integrity department or who is too self-absorbed to make the cut. Or so the test companies promise.

Beyond Background Checks

Concerned about the human investment they make when they hire employees, companies are increasingly turning to testing companies to help weed out undesirable applicants, even for entry-level jobs. Here are some questions from a test developed by John Kamp, an industrial psychologist, that is designed to identify employees who might be prone to on-the-job accidents.

CHECK YES OR NO	YES	NO
1. You like a lot of excitement in your life.	☐	☐
2. An employee who takes it easy at work is cheating his employer.	☐	☐
3. You are a cautious person.	☐	☐
4. In the past three years you have found yourself in a shouting match at school or work.	☐	☐
5. You like to drive fast just for fun.	☐	☐

Comprehension: Inference and Interpretation

Complete each sentence by circling the correct letter.

1. The purpose of the questions in the test on page 115 is to _____.

   a. eliminate people who would cause problems at work

   b. find people for entry-level jobs

   c. help employees understand themselves

2. The test-publishing companies _____.

   a. are controlled by the government

   b. have a lot of power

   c. are not financially successful

3. The author of this article is _____.

   a. against psychological tests for people applying for entry-level jobs

   b. in favor of psychological tests for people applying for entry-level jobs

   c. unsure of the quality of the tests that are being used today

Receptive Model

Listening with a Purpose

Determine Context

🎧 *Listen to the conversation. Then answer each question in your own words.*

1. What is the relationship between the speakers? _____

2. How often do they see each other? _____

3. What are they talking about? _____

Listening Between the Lines

🎧 *Now listen between the lines for the people's feelings. Circle the choice that correctly completes each statement in Column A.*

Column A

1. Allison (is / isn't) happy in her job.

2. Allison has (frequently / rarely) changed jobs.

3. Allison feels the job she's doing is (above / below) her ability.

4. Rob probably thinks there (is / isn't) such a thing as the perfect job.

5. Rob probably thinks it (would / wouldn't) be a good idea for Allison to look for another job.

Column B

a. "Again?"

b. "My skills aren't being used."

c. "I'll give it some thought."

d. "Every job has its ups and downs."

e. "I'd think twice before I left a sure thing."

f. "But basically it's the pits."

🎧 *Listen again to the conversation. Match each statement in Column A with a quotation from Column B that supports your choice. You will not use all the quotations in Column B.*

It depends.

In my opinion...

I'm for...

Rob says, "Every job has its ups and downs." Do you think there is such a thing as the right job or the perfect job? How would you describe a good job? Discuss your opinions with a partner.

I don't feel strongly about...   As far as I'm concerned...

What about you?

Game *(reinforces reported speech)*

Write three sentences about yourself. Write one about the past, one about the present, and one about the future. They can be true or false.

With a partner, play a game against another team of partners. Read a sentence to your partner. Your partner reports what you said, using reported speech.

The other team decides whether this statement is true or false. They earn a point for guessing correctly. The first team to earn 5 points wins.

Example: **Team 1** **A:** Last year I traveled to twenty-eight countries.

B: Brenda told me she'd traveled to twenty-eight countries last year.

Team 2 **C:** I doubt it. (*or* I don't believe it. *or* You've got to be kidding.)

Team 1 **A:** You're wrong. I <u>did</u> travel to twenty-eight countries.

Vocabulary

Jobs and Employment

 *Say each word or phrase. Study the definitions.*

employed: A person who has a job is **employed.**

unemployed: A person who wants a job but doesn't have one is **unemployed.**

self-employed: A person who earns a living by working in his or her own business and not for a company is **self-employed.**

get hired: A person who **gets hired** has a new job.

(continued on next page)

HE SAID HE'D MISSED HIS TRAIN. **117**

get fired: A person who **gets fired** loses a job.

a salary: A **salary** is an amount of money paid regularly for work, usually by the week, month, or year.

a paycheck: A **paycheck** is a check given to an employee as payment for work.

retire: To **retire** is to stop working, usually permanently.

a pension: A **pension** is money paid regularly to an employee after the employee retires.

benefits: Health insurance, life insurance, vacation pay, and a pension are **benefits.**

go bankrupt: When a company **goes bankrupt,** it doesn't have enough money to pay its expenses.

Vocabulary Practice

Complete the story. Fill in each blank with the correct vocabulary item.
Use each word or phrase only once.

This is the story of Janet. Two years ago she was _____. She hadn't
                                                                            1.

worked for several months and was almost out of money. Then somebody told her about a

job at a computer software company, and she went for an interview. The interview went very

well, and Janet _____ immediately. For the first several months, Janet was
                        2.

_____ as a temporary worker, but then the company put her on staff
        3.

and paid her a _____. The _____ were excellent. In
                    4.   **5.**

addition to her regular _____ every two weeks, Janet had a good health
                                6.

insurance plan, vacation pay, and a _____ for her old age. But then
                                            7.

something went wrong. The company had made some bad decisions, and soon it started

to lose money. Within two months, Janet and many other employees _____,
                                                                                8.

and a month after that the company _____. At first Janet didn't know
                                            9.

what to do, but then she had an idea. "Why don't I start my own business?" she thought.

She did that, and now she's a _____ software developer. She's her own
                                    10.

boss, and she's earning enough money to live comfortably. She's even earning enough to

save money for when she _____.
                                11.

In Your Own Words

▶ Speaking

Warm up: *Talk about the pictures with a partner.* • *What did the male interviewer think?* • *What did the female interviewer think?* • *What happened at the interviews?*

Then: *Create conversations for the people in one of the scenes. OR Talk about what happened after the interviews. Say as much as you can.*

Erin Lacy's Interview

Eva Kane's Interview

▶ Writing: An Essay

Write about the best or the worst job you've ever had. This can be a job that lasted a long time or a short time. It can be a paid or a volunteer job. Explain what you did and why this job was good or bad for you. OR Write about the kind of job you would like to have in the future. Explain why.

119

I'm so tired I don't really feel like going.

Warm up: What kind of music do you like best?
Listen. 🎧

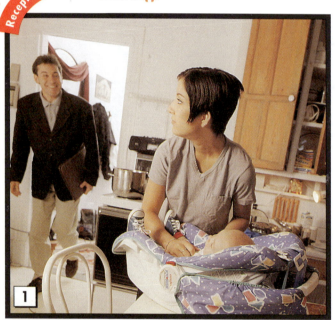

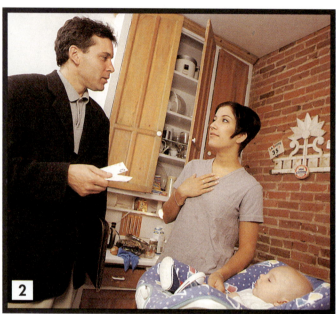

Comprehension: Understanding Meaning from Context

Listen to the conversation again. Match each underlined expression from the photo story with its meaning in Column B.

Column A

1. We need to <u>get going</u>.

2. <u>It slipped my mind</u>.

3. And these tickets <u>cost a bundle</u>.

4. I really don't want <u>to waste the other ticket</u>.

5. We don't have <u>much in common</u>.

Column B

a. many similar interests

b. were very expensive

c. not to use it

d. I forgot about it

e. leave soon

 **Tell a partner about Bill and his father-in-law. Use your own words. Say as much as you can.**

Reading Focus • A Newspaper Editorial

Before You Read: *Is music important in your life?*

Read the editorial. (Note the examples of gerunds and infinitives in bold type.) 🎧

The Times   **Editorial**

Bring Back Music in the Schools

by Hillary Chow, editor-in-chief

The school board has announced that, effective next year, the district will **stop providing** music instruction in the public schools. We at *The Times* feel this is the wrong decision, and we **urge** board members **to reconsider** their action.

Board officials say that the school **can** no longer **afford to hire** music teachers or **pay for** instruments. In these times of budget cuts, they say, music is a frill, a nice addition to the curriculum but not a necessary one. We disagree. The purpose of school is to educate students, not just to train them.

Ten years ago there was a strong music program in the schools in our city. All students were educated in vocal music, and all students had the option of **learning to play** a musical instrument for a year, with the school district lending students their instruments if their parents couldn't afford them. At the end of that year, students could either stop or **continue to study** their instrument. My own children participated in this program. At the end of the year, my daughter **quit to study** computers. That was her choice, but at least she had the experience. My son, however, **kept taking** music classes, and he later won a music scholarship to the university. With the school board's recent decision,

this sort of thing will no longer be a possibility. Our city will be the poorer for it.

We at *The Times* have seen a copy of the school board's budget for next year. We note that, while music is being eliminated, the amount of money available for athletic teams is being increased. Why are we spending so much on activities that benefit 20 percent of the students while spending nothing on a program that would benefit everyone? We don't **suggest getting rid of** all athletic teams. We do **suggest trying to achieve** a balance between sports and music. We calculate that, if the school board eliminated two sports and kept the others, there would be enough money to fund the entire music program.

The capacity to appreciate music is one of the defining characteristics of humanity. Music is everywhere. It's played in elevators. It's in the background of every movie, every TV program, almost every commercial. People of all ages and walks of life attend concerts. Music stores do a booming business. Music is something we all have in common, and it **allows** us **to express** ourselves. Doesn't it make sense for children to be educated about one of the central experiences of human culture?

Comprehension: Inference and Interpretation

The editorial says, "The purpose of school is to educate students, not just to train them . . . we suggest a balance between sports and music." What does this mean?

Gerunds and Infinitives after Certain Verbs

Gerunds are used as objects of certain verbs such as **avoid, consider, enjoy, feel like, keep, mind,** and **miss.** These verbs are never immediately followed by an infinitive.

               gerund

I **missed seeing** you yesterday.

Other verbs such as **decide, expect, manage, learn, need, pretend, seem, want,** and **would like** can be followed immediately by an infinitive. These verbs are never followed by a gerund. (See page 149 for a more complete list of verbs followed by gerunds and infinitives.)

               infinitive

I **want to thank** you for inviting me to the concert.

Some verbs such as **begin, can't stand, continue, hate, intend, like, love, prefer,** and **start** can be followed immediately by either a gerund or an infinitive without any change in meaning.

         gerund   infinitive

I **hate getting up** early.   I **hate to get up** early.

Be careful! Some verbs such as **forget, quit, regret, remember, stop,** and **try** can be followed immediately by either a gerund or an infinitive, but with a change in meaning.

              gerund

I **remember getting** the tickets. (I remember that I got them.)

            infinitive

I **remembered to get** the tickets. (I didn't forget to get them.)

TIP: Pay special attention to the verb **stop.**

     Helen **stopped playing** the piano. (She stopped the activity of playing the piano.)

     Helen **stopped to have** lunch. (She stopped doing another activity in order to have lunch.)

Remember that certain verbs such as **tell, encourage, invite, urge,** and **permit** are followed by a noun or pronoun object before an infinitive. (See page 149 for a more complete list of these verbs.)

           verb   object   infinitive

This school **encourages students to study** music.

GRAMMAR TASK: Find a sentence in the Reading Focus on page 122 in which an infinitive can be changed to a gerund. Rewrite the sentence with a gerund.

Grammar with a Partner

Ask your partner about the role of music in his or her life. Ask these questions. Take notes.

1. As a child, did you **enjoy** listening to music?

2. What kind of music did you **like** to listen to?

3. Did you and your parents listen to the same kind of music? If not, explain the differences. Do you ever **remember** disagreeing over music?

4. Did your taste in music change as you got older? In what way?

5. Did you ever **learn** to play an instrument? Which one?

| piano | guitar | saxophone | violin | drum | flute |

6. If yes, when did you **start** to play the instrument? Did you **mind** practicing? When did you **stop** taking lessons? Or do you still take lessons? If you no longer play the instrument, do you **miss** playing it?

7. If you didn't **learn** to play an instrument, **would** you **like** to learn one now? Which one?

Write a paragraph about the role of music in your partner's life. Use your notes.

SOCIAL LANGUAGE 1
How to make an excuse/suggest an alternative

Conversation

🎧 *Read and listen to the conversation.*

A: I don't know how I'll manage to get all this work done.

B: I'd help, but I'm <u>up to my ears in work</u>. I'm sure Jill wouldn't mind giving you a hand.

A: Isn't she busy with her job?

B: No. She usually has a lot of time on her hands around now.

A: Good idea. I'll <u>give her a ring</u>.

🎧 *Listen again and practice.*

Variations

I'm up to my ears in work.
I'm swamped.
I'm overwhelmed.
I'm too busy.

Variations

I'll give her a ring.
I'll call her.
I'll ask her.

Improvise

With a partner, improvise a conversation. One of you has too much to do and needs help. The other partner suggests something. Use the conversation as a model.

☑ **Now you know how to make an excuse. You also know how to suggest an alternative.**

HOW TO introduce new information

Conversation

🎧 *Read and listen to the conversation.*

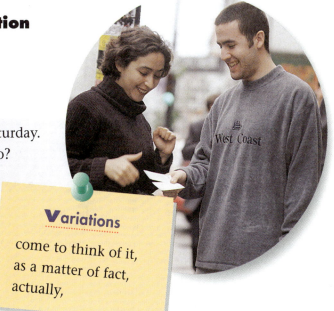

A: I've got an extra ticket for the opera on Saturday. Do you know anyone who might like to go?

B: Not offhand. But I'll ask around.

A: Thanks.

B: Hey, come to think of it, I'm free! I'd love to go.

A: Great. Do you mind driving?

B: Not at all. Pick you up at seven?

🎧 *Listen again and practice.*

Variations

come to think of it,
as a matter of fact,
actually,

Improvise

One partner has an extra ticket to an event and asks for help finding someone to take it. Use the conversation as a model.

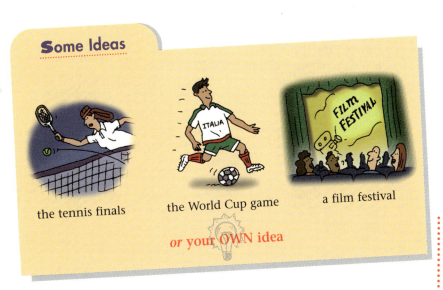

Some Ideas

the tennis finals

the World Cup game

a film festival

or your OWN idea

☑ **Now you know how to introduce new information.**

Authentic Reading

from *The New Book of Knowledge*

***B**efore You Read:* Do you know the Beatles' music? Do you like it?

Read the article. 🎧

BEATLES, THE

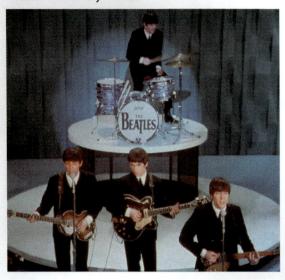

During most of the 1960's, the Western world seemed to move to the beat of four young rock musicians from Liverpool, England. They called themselves the Beatles.

John Lennon (1940–1980), a guitarist and singer, was the original leader of the group. He explained the name Beatles in this way: "When you said it, it was crawly things [beetles]; when you read it, it was beat music." The other members were Paul McCartney (1942–) and George Harrison (1943–), also guitarists and singers, and the drummer and singer Ringo Starr (1940–), whose real name was Richard Starkey.

Before the Beatles, many people thought rock was American music that was not to be taken seriously. The Beatles proved them wrong.

Each Beatle brought different strengths to the group. John had a strong personality and a sharp wit. Paul was a showman, who charmed audiences with his melodic voice. George was known as a gifted and serious musician. Ringo was adored for his "goofy," down-to-earth personality.

Brian Epstein, a young record dealer, became their manager. He was a major force in their success. With great difficulty, he found a record company willing to sign the Beatles. Their first single recording, "Love Me Do" (1962), quickly became popular. Their second record, "Please Please Me" (1963), was a big hit. Teenagers—in a frenzy known as "Beatlemania"—struggled to get close to their new heroes.

The Beatles appeared in New York for the first time in 1964. Their engaging personalities and energetic sound turned Britain's most popular rock group into an overnight success in the United States. Within weeks, the top five best-selling records there were all by the Beatles.

Before long, adults found it hard to ignore the Beatles' talent. In 1965, Queen Elizabeth II honored the Beatles by making them members of the Order of the British Empire.

As time went on, the words of their songs, written mainly by Lennon and McCartney, became more poetic. Their music changed, too. The Beatles began experimenting with electronic effects and instruments from around the world. And they invited jazz and classical musicians to perform on their recordings.

The Beatles made their last stage appearance in 1966. They produced their masterpiece, the album *Sergeant Pepper's Lonely Hearts Club Band*, in 1967, the year of their manager's death. Later that year, the four wrote and directed a film, *Magical Mystery Tour*, in which they toured the English countryside in search of wonder, magic, and fun.

In 1970 the group disbanded. All four continued to enjoy some success as solo artists during the 1970's. Many fans hoped for a reunion. But in 1980, John Lennon was assassinated in New York City. The "magical mystery tour" was truly over.

Comprehension: Factual Recall

*Mark each statement **true** or **false**, according to the reading. If a statement is false, change it to a true one.*

		True	False
1.	Ringo Starr, who was the Beatles' drummer, wanted to be known as Richard Starkey.	☐	☐
2.	It was with difficulty that Brian Epstein managed to find a company that would agree to produce the Beatles' first recording.	☐	☐
3.	In their early period, the Beatles began experimenting with different sounds and different instruments.	☐	☐
4.	The Beatles continued to work together until John Lennon's death in 1980.	☐	☐

Pronunciation
The Letter *h*

*Most words that begin with the letter **h** have a pronounced **"h"** sound. A few words that begin with **h** have a silent **"h"** sound.*

🎧 *Listen and repeat.*

pronounced "h" sound	**silent "h" sound**
how	hour
honey	honest
hair	heir

*Also, pronouns that begin with an **"h"** sound lose most or all of the sound when they occur in unstressed words.*

Example: Her hands are wet. Give ̸her a towel. ("Her" is stressed; "her" is unstressed.)

🎧 *Listen and repeat.*

He managed to see ̸her before she left home.
I felt like giving ̸him that handmade guitar.
He'll help ̸her in an ̸hour.

🎧 *Now listen and mark the places where the **h** is not pronounced.*

You should have shown him your CDs and let him borrow some.
What's her favorite song?
He bought her a ticket to that concert.

🎧 *Listen again and repeat.*

(reinforces gerunds and infinitives)

Game

Partner A, read this anecdote about the nineteenth-century German composer Brahms. Partner B, turn to page 143 and read the anecdote there. Take turns telling each other about the anecdote you read. Use your own words.

One day Johannes Brahms surprised his friends by announcing that he was going to stop composing music. He said, "I want to enjoy my life."

Several months passed. Then one day a new masterpiece of his was played in public.

"I thought you didn't want to write any more music," a friend said.

Brahms replied, "You're right, but after a few days of leisure I really relaxed. I didn't try to compose; the music just came to me without any effort."

Receptive Model

Listening with a Purpose

Determine Context

🎧 *Listen to the conversation. Then answer each question in your own words.*

1. What is the relationship between the people who are talking?

_____

2. Where are they?

_____

3. What are they talking about?

_____

Listening Between the Lines

🎧 **A.** *Listen between the lines for each speaker's point of view. Complete each sentence by circling the correct letter.*

Quotation

1. The father thinks rap _____.

   a. is dangerous   **b.** is not music   **c.** is too loud   _____

2. The daughter thinks classical music _____.

   a. isn't as exciting   **b.** is hard to   **c.** is interesting   _____
      as rap   appreciate

3. The mother thinks heavy metal music _____.

   a. can hurt your   **b.** is not real   **c.** is boring   _____
      health   music

4. The mother thinks music _____ she was a teenager.

   a. has gotten   **b.** has gotten   **c.** is about the same   _____
      better since   worse since   quality as when

B. *Finally, read the following quotations from the conversation. With a partner, choose one quotation to support each answer in Listening Between the Lines on page 128. Write the letter of the quotation in the space provided.*

a. "Music wasn't this bad when we were teenagers, was it?"

b. "It wakes you up—gives you energy."

c. "Yeah, Nate. Find some music."

d. "None of you know what's good."

e. "I don't feel like losing my hearing tonight."

f. "Maybe every generation thinks what it likes is the best."

g. "This is what I want to listen to."

h. "Classical puts you to sleep."

Bonus Listening

🎧 *Read and listen to the* True Colors *song.*

You've got a mind full of dreams that are big as the open sky
And ideas that won't let you sleep.
If you want to stretch those wings and prove that you can fly,
Use your own words to set your ideas free.
And let your true colors come shining through.
Show your true colors, words that say what you want to.
So don't be afraid to let them show.
Your true colors, true colors, are beautiful like a rainbow.

Heart to Heart

🎧 *Now listen again to the* True Colors *song. What does "true colors" mean to you? What do you think "Let your true colors come shining through" means? Compare opinions with a partner.*

Vocabulary

Musical Terms

🎧 *Look at the pictures. Say each word or phrase.*

an orchestra

a band

a conductor

tuning a guitar

(continued on next page)

string instruments percussion instruments wind instruments keyboard instruments

classical music   popular music /   a vocalist   a chorus
                       pop music

Vocabulary Practice

Look at the pictures. Fill in each blank with the correct vocabulary item.

1. A kind of music that many people like is called _____.

2. Instruments whose sound is produced by touching or moving strings are called _____.

3. A(n) _____ is an individual singer.

4. Instruments whose sound is produced by hitting one object against another are called _____.

5. Instruments whose sound is produced by pushing down keys are called _____.

6. Instruments whose sound is produced by blowing air into them are called _____.

7. A kind of music (especially European music of the eighteenth and nineteenth centuries) that is often played by an orchestra is called _____.

8. A group of musicians who play wind, percussion, and keyboard instruments but generally not stringed instruments is called a(n) _____.

9. A group of people who sing together is called a(n) _____.

10. To adjust a musical instrument so that it plays correctly is to _____ it.

11. A person who leads an orchestra is called a(n) _____.

12. A group of musicians who play different instruments, including strings, is called a(n) _____.

▶ Speaking

Warm up: With a partner, look at the pictures. • What is the woman with the extra ticket trying to do? • Talk about the orchestra and the instruments.

Then: Create conversations for the people in the pictures. OR Talk about the people in the audience. Say as much as you can.

▶ Writing: An Essay about Music

Write about a song you really like. Try to explain why you like it. How does it make you feel? Do you associate the song with a certain person or time in your life?

Review, SelfTest, and Extra Practice

▶ **P**art 1

Review

We've Never Been on a Cruise Before.

🎧 *Listen to the conversation.*

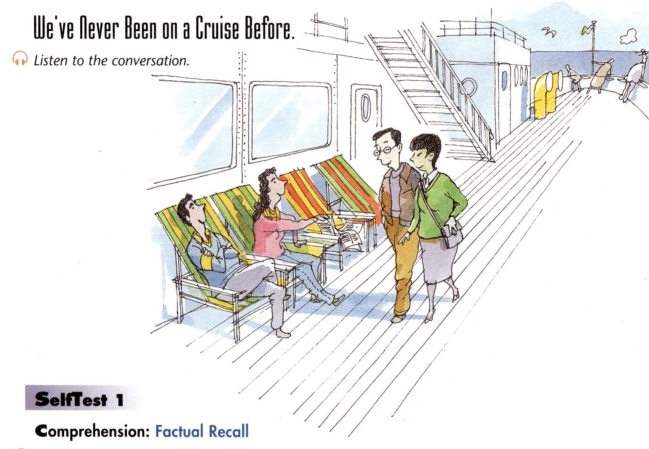

SelfTest 1

Comprehension: Factual Recall

🎧 *Listen to the conversation again. Then complete the statements in your own words.*

1. Yoshi and Megumi have never _____

_____.

2. Two years ago Alberto and Alicia _____

_____.

3. The first seating is at _____

_____.

4. The two couples plan _____

_____.

SelfTest 2

Grammar: Quoted Speech and Reported Speech

Change the quoted speech to reported speech.

Quoted Speech	**Reported Speech**
1. Megumi: "It's good to meet you."	Megumi told Alberto and Alicia _____.
2. Yoshi: "We've never been on a cruise before."	Yoshi said _____ _____.
3. Yoshi: "We're from Nagano, Japan."	Yoshi told them _____ _____.
4. Megumi: "No. Six is pretty early for us."	Megumi told him _____ _____.
5. Alicia: "We can continue our conversation."	Alicia said _____ _____.
6. Yoshi: "We'll meet you in the club room about nine-thirty."	Yoshi said _____ _____.

Grammar with a Partner

Improvise a conversation with a partner. You are traveling and have just met. Introduce yourselves and ask each other general questions. (You may want to give yourselves new identities. For example, you may want to be famous people.) Then make plans to meet later to continue talking.

Next, you and your partner talk to new partners. Tell your new partner about the person you've just met. Tell who he or she is and what he or she has told you.

Extra Practice

Part 2

Review

Authentic Reading
from Princess Cruises brochure

Before You Read: If you were going to take a cruise, what information would you want?

Read some helpful hints from a cruise brochure. 🎧

HELPFUL HINTS

MEALS: While aboard Princess ships, all meals are included (except alcoholic beverages). While ashore and on cruise tours, no other meals are included unless specified in the daily tour itinerary.

DINING ROOM: Passenger dining assignments are made by request on a first-come, first-served basis. To request preference in first or second seating, special diets, or seating with a specific party, have your travel agent make the arrangements at the time of booking. Approximate seating times while at sea are as follows: Breakfast—**first** 7:30am, **second** 8:30am; Lunch—**first** 12 Noon, **second** 1:30pm; Dinner—**first** 6:00pm, **second** 8:00pm.

CLOTHING SUGGESTIONS: Shipboard attire is mainly casual or semiformal and occasionally formal. Casual is appropriate for daytime aboard ship or ashore and consists of standard sports outfits as worn at resorts. Shoes should be low-heeled for deck activities. Evening attire on the cruise falls into 3 categories: casual, semiformal and formal. On casual evenings, open neck shirts, slacks and sports outfits are

appropriate. On semiformal evenings, ladies usually wear dresses or pantsuits; men wear coats and ties. On formal evenings, women usually wear evening gowns or cocktail dresses. Men wear tuxedos, dinner jackets or dark suits.

TIPPING: A 15% gratuity is automatically included on all beverage tabs for your convenience. You may also wish to reward your stateroom steward or stewardess and your dining room waiting staff with a cash tip.

TRAVELER'S CHECKLIST: When packing you should include: spare eyeglasses and contact lenses, sunglasses, extra film and camera batteries, prescription medicines, your address book, proof of citizenship, an umbrella and even binoculars.

Source: Excerpt from cruise brochure courtesy of Princess Cruises.

SelfTest 1

Comprehension: Factual Recall

Complete each statement in Column A with the letter of the correct choice from Column B.

Column A	Column B
1. Unless it is a formal evening, _____.	**a.** seats are given on a first-come, first-served basis
2. It is a good idea to make your dining room reservation as soon as possible because _____.	**b.** none are included on land unless specially noted
3. Unless you make a reservation in advance, _____.	**c.** you won't be able to sit with people you choose
4. Although all meals are included on the ship, _____.	**d.** women do not wear evening gowns or cocktail dresses

SelfTest 2

Grammar: Gerunds and Infinitives

Complete each sentence with the verb in parentheses and a gerund or an infinitive.

Would you _____ three gourmet meals a day? Wouldn't you _____
   1. (enjoy) eat   **2.** (love) dance

nightly under the stars? Or perhaps you _____ a spectacular sunset from your
                              3. (would like) watch

comfortable deck chair? In the morning you may _____ our aerobics classes or
                                    4. (feel like) attend

dance lessons. And at night you won't _____ our spectacular shows.
                         5. (want) miss

   All this and more is available to you on True Colors Cruises. _____ early
                                                   6. (Remember) book

because we fill up quickly. You won't ever _____ this vacation of a lifetime.
                            7. (regret) take

Call your travel agent today.

riting

You are on a cruise. Write a letter to a friend, telling all about it. Use the Authentic Reading on page 134 for ideas.

Part 3

Review

Would You Have Moved If You'd Known What It Would Be Like?

🎧 *Listen to the conversation.*

Comprehension: Factual Recall

🎧 *Read these statements. Then listen again for facts about the two couples. Complete each sentence by circling the correct letter.*

1. Alberto and Alicia moved to Brasilia because _____.

    a. Alicia had a job opportunity

    b. Alberto had a job opportunity

    c. they both had job opportunities

2. Alicia works as _____.

    a. a writer

    b. a teacher

    c. an editorial assistant

3. Alicia's father died _____.

    a. while she was in Chile

    b. before she could return to Chile

    c. while she was in Japan

4. Alicia speaks _____.

    a. Spanish and English

    b. English and Portuguese

    c. English, Spanish, and Portuguese

5. If Alberto and Alicia had known what their life in Brazil would be like, they _____.

    a. wouldn't have gone to Brazil

    b. might not have gone to Brazil

    c. would still have gone to Brazil

Bonus Question: What does Alicia mean when she says, "We've really had a chance to expand our horizons"?

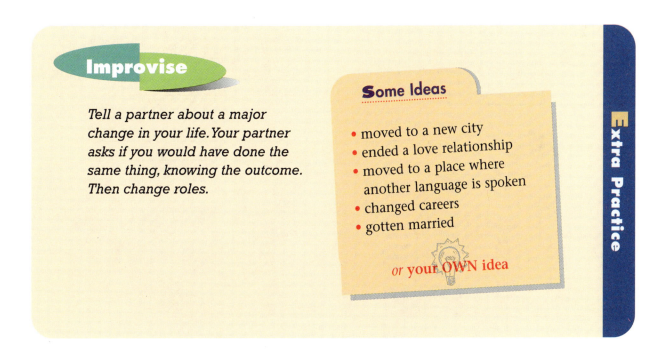

Improvise

Tell a partner about a major change in your life. Your partner asks if you would have done the same thing, knowing the outcome. Then change roles.

Some Ideas

• moved to a new city
• ended a love relationship
• moved to a place where another language is spoken
• changed careers
• gotten married

or your OWN idea

Extra Practice

SOCIAL LANGUAGE Review

Review 1

🎧 *Read and listen to this conversation in the ship's dining room.*

Improvise

You have an extra ticket for an event. Talk to a partner about the event and about your ticket. See if your partner knows someone who would like the ticket. Use the conversation as a model.

Review 2

🎧 *Read and listen to the conversation.*

A: Well, how did the tryout go?

B: Piece of cake.

A: So I guess you're pretty sure you're in the talent show?

B: No doubt about it.

A: Congratulations.

B: Actually, anyone who wants to be in it can.

A: Did you see any of the others? How were they?

B: Super. There was one woman who danced as well as any professional.

A: No kidding.

B: And there was this older guy who was hilarious.

A: Really?

B: Yeah. We were rolling in the aisles. I think you saw him at breakfast. He's the one whose wife is the ship's doctor.

A: Oh, I remember him, the guy who always wears a gray baseball cap, right?

B: That's right.

A: Well, I can't wait for the show.

Improvise

Improvise a conversation with a partner. One of you has tried out for a competition, a talent show, or a sports team. The other asks how it went and about the other contestants. Use the conversation as a model.

SOCIAL LANGUAGE SelfTest

Circle the appropriate statement or question to complete each of the following conversations.

1. A: _____

    B: What's the problem?

       a. Come to think of it, I'm free.

       b. Feel free to call on me anytime.

       c. There's something I'd like to talk to you about.

2. A: I'd like to return this can opener. It doesn't work.

    B: _____

       a. I'm sorry. Would you like to exchange it?

       b. That's OK. It's not that serious.

       c. Excuse me. I forgot all about it.

3. A: _____

    B: You're right. I'm sorry.

       a. You promised to help, but you're not helping.

       b. Will you promise to help?

       c. I promise to help out.

4. A: Why can't you stand it?

    B: _____

       a. What bothers me the most is the color.

       b. I really like the way the artist uses color.

       c. The color really grabs me.

5. A: Can you think of the name of the actor who played in *Gandhi?*

    B: _____

       a. Yes. Just come on over. I'll help you out.

       b. Yes. I can't wait to see him.

       c. Yes. Just give me a second. It's on the tip of my tongue.

6. A: _____

    B: Yes. I told everyone to meet in front of the language school.

       a. How did it go?

       b. All in all, I like it.

       c. Are we all set?

7. A: What do you think of this photograph?

   B: _____

   a. I can see what you mean.

   b. I think so, too.

   c. What I like most is the color contrast.

8. A: How did it go?

   B: _____

   a. It went well, all in all.

   b. Not offhand. But I'll ask around.

   c. It's all right.

9. A: _____

   B: No, but if I think of something, I'll let you know.

   a. Would you like to help?

   b. Is there anything I can do to help?

   c. Do I need help?

10. A: Can you believe he made that awful remark?

   B: _____

   a. I've got it.

   b. It's on the tip of my tongue.

   c. I would've told him to mind his own business.

11. A: _____

   B: I'd help, but I'm up to my ears in work.

   a. I don't know how I'll manage.

   b. I have a lot of time on my hands.

   c. How may I help you?

12. A: _____

   B: OK. I'll give him a ring.

   a. Frank's busy.

   b. Frank's away.

   c. Frank's got a lot of time on his hands.

Activity Links

Unit 1

Inter-Action

Partner B

Listen to Partner A's sentences about famous people. Then read a matching sentence that identifies each of the six famous people.

a. Julie Andrews had grown up in a musical family in England, and this musical background served her well in productions such as *My Fair Lady* and *Mary Poppins*.

b. John Paul II had been a priest for thirty-two years when he was named Pope in 1978.

c. By the time Mother Teresa was awarded the Nobel Peace Prize in 1979, she had already been helping the poor in India for thirty-one years

d. When Britain's Princess Diana died at the age of thirty-six in 1997, her friend Elton John reworked the song he had written for Marilyn Monroe—"Candle in the Wind"—and sang it at Diana's funeral.

e. His name, Buddha, means "Enlightened One" in the Sanskrit language. He founded the religion known as Buddhism around 530 B.C.

f. When Muhummad Ali won the world heavyweight boxing championship in 1964, he had already won the Olympic light-heavyweight championship.

Unit 3

Grammar with a Partner

Partner B

Read these sentences to Partner A. Partner A will respond with a conclusion.

a. I told a joke and nobody laughed.
b. I sent my friend a gift, and she still hasn't thanked me.
c. Kate is wearing a very big emerald ring today.

Partner A

Read these sentences to Partner B. Partner B will respond with a conclusion.

d. Emily got a ticket for speeding.
e. Sarah has been waiting outside her house for several hours.
f. She never calls me by my name.

Unit 3

Inter-Action

Answers

1. George and Rachel must have been fish.
2. The pilot must have been his sister.
3. Marie must have been too short to reach the button for the tenth floor.
4. He must have asked, "Which road do I take to your village?" If the woman was telling the truth, she would direct him to Choo, because that's where she would be from. If the woman was from Fink, she would lie and therefore point him to Choo.

Inter-Action

Partner B

Listen as Partner A reads the beginning of three proverbs. Then read the matching ending for each one.

1. _____, no one believes it.

2. _____, it will never pay more.

3. _____ until they hatch.

Now read the beginning of each of these proverbs to Partner A. Partner A will read the matching ending.

4. If people are worth knowing at all, _____.

5. The punishment of the liar is that he is not believed, _____.

6. Though people forget how fast you did a job, _____.

Game

Partner B

Read this anecdote about the late nineteenth-century Austrian composer Gustave Mahler. Then tell it to your partner. Use your own words.

Gustave Mahler hated to wake up early. He enjoyed working at night and sleeping during the day. One day Mahler received a notice to appear in court as a witness at 7:00 A.M. On the day of his court appearance, he overslept. The same thing happened a second time. Mahler got a third notice. But this time it said if he didn't appear, he would be thrown in jail for contempt of court.

A friend of Mahler's decided to help him. He came to Mahler's apartment and managed to get the composer dressed and ready in time for court.

As Mahler stepped outside early in the morning, he looked around and was amazed to see crowds of people up and around. He turned to his friend and asked in amazement, "Do all these people need to appear in court?"

Appendices

Key Vocabulary

This list represents key words and expressions presented in Book 4.

Unit 1

Nouns

Names

given name
surname
middle name
pseudonym

nickname
title
senior
junior
alias

Adjective

named after (for)

Expressions

To acknowledge an introduction

It's a pleasure to meet you.

To describe a relationship

be on a first-name basis

Other expressions

for short
As far as I'm concerned . . .
I don't feel strongly about . . .

Unit 2

Nouns

Family dynamics

siblings
sibling rivalry
only child
chores
orphan
birth parents
adoptive parents

Other nouns

apology
regret

Verbs

adopt
could have
should have
apologize

Expressions

To express regret

feel awful
be sorry

To reassure someone

Don't let it get to you.
You couldn't have known.

Other expressions

get angry
be upset
get divorced

Unit 3

Nouns

All about mystery

mystery
private investigators
clue
whodunit

Verbs

investigate
solve
must have
may have
might have
disappear

Adjectives

mysterious
suspenseful
unsolved
puzzled

Expressions

To speculate about possibilities

jump to conclusions

Other expressions

take something by mistake
reach someone
get in touch with someone
be on-line

Unit 4

Nouns

Scientific research

discovery
invention
construction
conclusion
experiment
hypothesis
patent
research
analysis

Verbs

Scientific research

discover
invent
construct
conclude
experiment
hypothesize
patent
do research
analyze

Modals

can
could
shall
should
ought to
had better
may
might
will
would
must

Adjectives

controversial
skeptical

Expressions

To express an opinion

If you ask me, ...
Personally, I think ...
In my opinion, ...
The bad outweighs the good.
The disadvantages outweigh the advantages.
The dangers outweigh the benefits.

To express skepticism

I wouldn't hold my breath.

Unit 5

Nouns

People who perform services

orthodontist
plastic surgeon
typist
tailor
interior decorator
mechanic

plumber
locksmith
accountant

Other noun

clinic

Verbs

Services

tune up
install

alter
repair
shorten
take in
let out
check out

Expressions

To state a problem

have a hard time doing something

have trouble doing something

To ask for a favor

help someone out
mind asking someone to do something

To give advice about having something done

It's (not) worth it.

Unit 6

Nouns

Sleep and dreams

early bird
night owl
light sleeper
heavy sleeper
nightmare
insomnia

To ask for a refund

refund
credit

Verbs

Sleep and dreams

snore
daydream

To ask for a refund

return
exchange

Pronouns

Relative pronouns

who
whose
whom

that
which

Expressions

Sleep and dreams

take a nap

To remind someone

If you recall, ...
It's just that ...

Unit 7

Noun

souvenir

Verb

recall

Adjectives

Memory

absent-minded
memorable

Expressions

To confirm information

You mean that?
Are you sure?
Really?

To express trouble remembering something

I'm drawing a blank.
It's slipped my mind.
I can't think of it.
I've forgotten.
My mind went blank.
It's on the tip of my tongue

To describe ways of memorizing

learn something by heart
learn something by association

Unit 8

Nouns

Art

sculptor
sculpture
sketch
easel
portrait
landscape
still life
subject
model

Adjective

abstract

Conjunctions

To tell under what conditions

if
unless

To tell why

because
since

To tell when

when
whenever
before
after
until

To present a contrast

although
though
even though

Expressions

To explain what you like about something

What I like most . . .
What's really great . . .
What really grabs me . . .

To explain what you don't like about something

What bothers me the most . . .
What I don't like . . .
What turns me off . . .
What I hate . . .

To acknowledge another point of view

I can see what you mean.

To arrange something

Are we all set?

Unit 9

Nouns

Jobs and employment

salary
paycheck
pension
benefits
interview

Verbs

Jobs and employment

retire
interview

Adjectives

Jobs and employment

employed
unemployed
self-employed

Expressions

Jobs and employment

get hired
get fired
go bankrupt

To summarize

all in all
on the whole
considering
overall

To express confidence

Super.
Great.
Piece of cake.
Fantastic.

Other expression

be supposed to

Unit 10

Nouns

Music

popular / pop music
classical music
string instruments
percussion instruments
keyboard instruments
wind instruments
conductor
band
orchestra
chorus
vocalist

Verb

tune an instrument

Expressions

To be very busy

I'm up to my ears (in work).
I'm swamped.
I'm overwhelmed.
I'm too busy.

To express sudden remembering

Come to think of it, . . .
As a matter of fact, . . .
Actually, . . .

Other expressions

give someone a hand
have time on one's hands
give someone a ring
ask around
Not offhand.

Common Irregular Verbs

The following list is provided for reference. Not all of these verbs appear in *True Colors*.

Base Form	Simple Past	Past Participle
be	was, were	been
beat	beat	beaten
become	became	become
begin	began	begun
bend	bent	bent
bet	bet	bet
bite	bit	bitten
blow	blew	blown
break	broke	broken
bring	brought	brought
build	built	built
buy	bought	bought
*can	could	been able to
catch	caught	caught
choose	chose	chosen
come	came	come
cost	cost	cost
cut	cut	cut
deal	dealt	dealt
dig	dug	dug
do	did	done
draw	drew	drawn
drink	drank	drunk
drive	drove	driven
eat	ate	eaten
fall	fell	fallen
feed	fed	fed
feel	felt	felt
fight	fought	fought
fit	fit, fitted	fit, fitted
fly	flew	flown
forget	forgot	forgotten
forgive	forgave	forgiven
freeze	froze	frozen
get	got	gotten
give	gave	given
go	went	gone
grind	ground	ground
grow	grew	grown
hang	hung, hanged	hung, hanged
have	had	had
hear	heard	heard
hide	hid	hidden
hit	hit	hit
hold	held	held
hurt	hurt	hurt
keep	kept	kept
know	knew	known
lead	led	led
leave	left	left

* *Can* is a modal.

(continued on next page)

Base Form	Simple Past	Past Participle
lend	lent	lent
let	let	let
light	lit, lighted	lit, lighted
lose	lost	lost
make	made	made
mean	meant	meant
meet	met	met
*must	had to	had to
put	put	put
quit	quit	quit
read	read	read
ride	rode	ridden
ring	rang	rung
rise	rose	risen
run	ran	run
say	said	said
see	saw	seen
sell	sold	sold
send	sent	sent
set	set	set
sing	sang	sung
shake	shook	shaken
shoot	shot	shot
show	showed	shown
shrink	shrank	shrunk
shut	shut	shut
sit	sat	sat
sleep	slept	slept
slide	slid	slid
speak	spoke	spoken
speed	sped	sped
spend	spent	spent
spread	spread	spread
stand	stood	stood
steal	stole	stolen
stick	stuck	stuck
sting	stung	stung
strike	struck	struck
swear	swore	sworn
sweep	swept	swept
swim	swam	swum
swing	swung	swung
take	took	taken
teach	taught	taught
tear	tore	torn
tell	told	told
think	thought	thought
throw	threw	thrown
understand	understood	understood
wake	woke	woken
wear	wore	worn
win	won	won
wind	wound	wound
write	wrote	written

* *Must* is a modal.

Gerunds and Infinitives

Common Verbs Followed by the Gerund (verb + *-ing*)

advise	consider	finish	mind	quit
appreciate	discuss	give up	miss	recall
avoid	dislike	imagine	practice	recommend
can't help	enjoy	keep	prohibit	suggest
can't stand	feel like	mention	propose	

Common Verbs Followed by the Infinitive (*to* + base form of verb)

agree	can('t) afford	learn	plan	refuse
appear	decide	manage	prepare	seem
attempt	expect	need	pretend	want
begin	hope	offer	promise	would like

Common Verbs Followed by the Gerund or the Infinitive

begin	forget*	like	quit*	start
can't stand	hate	love	regret*	stop*
continue	intend	prefer	remember*	try*

There is a significant difference in meaning between the two forms.

Verbs Followed by Object + Infinitive

Example: I asked	advise	encourage	order	remind
her to help me.	allow	force	permit	teach
	ask*	invite	persuade	tell
	convince			urge

The verb ask *can also be followed by the infinitive without an object (Bill* asked *to leave).*

Adjectives and Adverbs

Regular

Adjective	Adverb
actual	actually
bad	badly
careful	carefully
careless	carelessly
clear	clearly
easy	easily
fortunate	fortunately
general	generally
happy	happily
normal	normally
quick	quickly
rapid	rapidly
real	really
sincere	sincerely
slow	slowly
true	truly
usual	usually

Irregular

Adjective	Adverb
early	early
fast	fast
good	well
hard	hard

Grammatical Terms

present continuous	I'**m making** dinner right now.
simple present tense	Eric **likes** hamburgers.
past tense of *be*	I **was** at work yesterday.
simple past tense	We **played** soccer last weekend.
habitual past (no longer true)	I **used to play** tennis, but I don't anymore.
past continuous	I **was sleeping** when the phone rang.
present perfect	I'**ve had** the flu for three days.
present perfect continuous	Karen **has been looking** for you.
past perfect	By the time Ed got home, he **had missed** dinner.
real conditional	**If** I **have** time, I'**ll visit** you.
present unreal conditional ————	**If** I **had** a car, I **wouldn't take** the bus to work.
past unreal conditional	**If** it **hadn't rained**, we **would have gone** to the picnic.
the future with *be going to*	We'**re going to see** a play tonight.
the future with *have to*	Alice **has to work** tomorrow.
the future with the present continuous	I'**m studying** tomorrow.
the future with *will*	Sam **will arrive** next week.
base form	Can I help you **type** your paper?
definite article	About fifty people came to **the** meeting.
indefinite article	They took the man to **a** hospital nearby.
infinitive	I want **to go** home.
gerund	Alex hates **driving**.
noun	That **restaurant** has great **food**.
verb	Sheila **runs** five miles a day.
adjective	That's a **beautiful** hat.
adverb	Amber speaks **quietly**.
present participle	Don is **reading** that book.
past participle	I haven't **seen** that movie yet.
the causative	I'm going to **have** the mechanic **fix** my car.
the passive causative	Jack finally **got/had** the TV **repaired**.
adjective clause	The woman **that I called** is the supervisor.
reduced adjective clause	The woman **I called** is the supervisor.
adverbial clause	I'll leave **when the meeting is over**.
quoted speech	Helen said, **"I want to go to the party."**
reported speech	Helen said **she wanted to go to the party.**
modal	He **must** have missed his plane.

The Passive Voice

Passive Voice

This class **is taught** by Ms. Davis.
"The Moonlight Sonata" **was composed** by Beethoven.
Lunch **will be served** at 1:00.
Lunch **is being served** in the cafeteria this week.
Lunch **was being served** when the lights went out.
None of the criminals **have been caught**.
When I heard the news last night, none of the criminals **had been caught**.

Modal Passive

Rice **cannot be grown** in cold climates.

(Active Voice)

Ms. Davis **teaches** this class.